Public Education for Our Nation's Democracy

Commentaries on Schooling in America

David C. Berliner

Foreword by P. David Pearson

Teachers College Press

Teachers College, Columbia University

Published by Teachers College Press, 1234 Amsterdam Avenue, New York, NY 10027

Copyright © 2025 by Teachers College, Columbia University

Architectural lintel by Alin Gavriliuc / Unsplash. Linen texture by Amandaaaaaaaa / Pexels.

Library of Congress Cataloging-in-Publication Data is available at loc.gov

ISBN 978-0-8077-8722-9 (paper)
ISBN 978-0-8077-8723-6 (hardcover)
ISBN 978-0-8077-8316-0 (ebook)

Printed on acid-free paper
Manufactured in the United States of America

23 22 21 20 19 18 17 16   8 7 6 5 4 3 2 1

TECHNOLOGY, EDUCATION—CONNECTIONS
THE TEC SERIES

Series Editor: Marcia C. Linn
Advisory Board: Robert Bjork, Chris Dede, Joseph Krajcik, Carol Lee,
Jim Minstrell, Jonathan Osborne, Mitch Resnick, Constance Steinkuehler

Contents

Foreword

Choose your metaphor, adage, or maxim to characterize the contributions of David Berliner to our public discourse on educational policy. Many fit! Across a long and distinguished career as an educational psychologist, school-based researcher, and educational policy analyst, David has

- Spoken truth to power!
- Told it like it is!
- Noted that the emperor has no clothes!

Wherever and whenever he sees hypocrisy or a betrayal of public education, he is not shy about telling us where he stands on that issue and why.

Rare among educational researchers, David's prose speaks as forcefully and transparently to the average citizen (and voter) as it does to his fellow scholars. This, his most recent effort, *Public Education for Our Nation's Democracy*, will sit comfortably on our bookcase of policy commentaries, alongside his earlier classics as a must-read text for those of us who care about the plight of public education.

This new volume presents a diverse set of self-contained essays on various aspects of teaching, learning, and schooling that are important to David. Fortunately for us, his readers, they also matter to us.

David must be an avid reader of high quality journalism. Why? Because he is a master at using what feature writers call the hook—the compelling anecdote or case—that highlights the issue for which he seeks our undivided attention. He compels us to care about the issues and the people portrayed in the story so that we will read to find out how the matter can be fixed, or at least rendered less damaging.

What awaits you inside the covers of this new classic? I'll share a few of my favorite essays, though you won't want to skip a single one! The good thing about free-standing essays is that the order doesn't matter much. I've tried several orders in preparing this foreword. They all seem to work!

- *Essay 3.* The first long essay in the book focuses on interest and begins, as many essays written by grandfathers do, with a pithy and compelling anecdote about a brilliant grandchild. In David's case, the hero is David's 11-year-old grandson, MacKenzie the Magnificent. MacKenzie has mastered the rules, moves, and substantive knowledge of a deeply complex card game, Magic, which, as it turns out, proves challenging to Grandpa. The point of the essay is simple and powerful: When it comes to predicting future learning, both IQ and knowledge have important roles, but so does motivation, especially in the form of deep personal interest in a topic or practice. And often, interest will compensate for still-developing cognitive skill and even knowledge in shaping learning about even the most complex of domains.

- *Essay 5*. Here David takes on unconscionable practice, perpetrated mainly by charter and private schools, in which school officials "cream off" the most able and well-prepared students or "cull out" the least able and ill-prepared students, leaving it to the public schools to provide services for those students they choose not to serve or deal with in any meaningful way.

- *Essay 13*. Unlike his push for the arts in Essay 14, which is based on the power of arts for art's sake to enhance the quality of one's life, David's push for soft skills (taking responsibility, industriousness, leadership, or developing well-rounded interests of the sort one finds in extracurricular activities) is based on their capacity to predict (and maybe impact) job success and income after. The lesson to parents: Make sure your kids get opportunities to develop these dispositions in everyday home and community settings.

- *Essay 14*. This is a different take on multiculturalism, intentionally so. Starting from the premise that cultural relevance (kids should see themselves and their communities in the curriculum) and cultural diversity (kids should see others in the curriculum to broaden their world views) are both important and empirically valid, David argues for *Ars Gratia Artis*—art for art's sake—high culture from any, many, and all subcultures within a society, as well as imported arts from other countries and cultures.

- *Essay 16*. Here, David describes the "cohort" effect on achievement perpetrated by housing segregation. Put simply, the cohort effect shows that the average social class served by a school (who lives in the neighborhood) affects an individual's achievement even more than the social class of that individual's family.

Let me stop with these five essays, lest I end up summarizing them all and leaving little for you, the reader, to discover on your own. Suffice it to say that the remaining 13 essays are equally as important, compelling, and provocative as those I have singled out.

Considered as a whole, the themes that emerge across the essays are consistent with the book's title: *Public Education for Our Nation's Democracy*.

If we want a democratic society in which an informed citizenry, equipped with knowledge and critical reasoning skills, elects and ousts politicians who make our policies, then a well-funded, well-supported public education system—one in which we can all take great pride—is an absolute necessity. And initiatives like charter schools, skimming the best students, or segregating by race or class must be stopped, period.

I'll close with a few predictions about the potential reactions to the book and its ultimate place in the grand library of the educational policy world. First, like David's other work, this book will be read by future generations who want to know what drove the policy of the first quarter of the 21st Century. Second, it will attract both admirers and critics. The admirers will be (a) progressive educators who value student-centered over curriculum-centered schools, (b) advocates—both liberal and conservative—of public schools as the crucible of preparation for participation in a democratic society, and (c) educators who value diversity, equity, inclusion and, above all, fair-mindedness in our schools and society. Critics will be mainly (a) traditionalists who want all schools (indeed, all Americans) to value mostly white, mostly male, mostly Christian cultural traditions in both society and schooling, and (b) the current MAGA radicals who want to replace 90% of what is in school curricula, ban 80% of what is in school libraries, and redirect untethered public funds to private schooling. This book will not be ignored! For different reasons, neither the progressives nor the traditionalists can afford to.

—*P. David Pearson*

Introduction

My career has been that of an educational researcher. My specialty was the study of K-12 classroom teaching and educational policy. After my doctorate was awarded at Stanford University, I cowrote a well-regarded textbook, wrote journal articles, edited a handbook on educational psychology, delivered academic papers at conferences all around the world, taught in many countries, and consulted frequently with schools and departments of education in the United States and abroad. But the professional activity I enjoyed the most was to occasionally visit classrooms and schools, in different states and countries, and try to make sense of them.

Why are things the way they are? Why did teacher X do one thing with Johnny, but changed her behavior when she worked with Janie? How did teacher Y know when his class was "getting it," and when they were not? Why do some teachers burn out in a few years while others enjoy their professional lives enormously over many years? What do different teachers do with kids who seem to refuse to learn, or who are absent a lot, or have no money for the school lunch?

I always thought it strange that one of the founding fathers of my field of educational psychology, E. L. Thorndike of Teachers College at Columbia, told his graduate students not to bother going into classrooms to study learning in real schools. He said classrooms were much too complex, and rather boring! Over a half century later, 1968, at the University of Chicago, another educational psychologist, Philip Jackson, wrote a book called *Life in Classrooms*. He also pointed out how incredibly complex classrooms were. It was scholars like these, discussing the complexity of classrooms, that attracted me and led me to spend a great deal of my time as a professional educator in real schools with their complex classrooms.

I liked visiting classrooms and schools to learn how they functioned—or didn't! I developed enormous respect for classroom teachers, the vast majority of whom were doing amazingly well, often with too little personal or fiscal support, frequently with complex family lives outside of school, and sometimes with students who really didn't want to be there, some of whom were quite dysfunctional cognitively or emotionally. The first essay I wrote, also the first in this collection, exists because I was so impressed with one of

1

the first teachers I visited. When I left her classroom, I was compelled to write down what I had experienced. I didn't want to forget what I had witnessed.

After that, when I witnessed or participated in some educational activity worth documenting, I wrote an essay. These were originally just for me, rather than for my colleagues. But now, in retirement, I have polished these a bit to share with others. That polishing was accomplished with the help of my dear friend, the influential scholar and incredible editor Gene V Glass and some of the staff at Teachers College Press. They have my thanks.

Essays are quite different from the professional research papers that I have done for so many years. But I am delighted to share 18 of these with you. They record what I was seeing in classrooms, or thinking about, over many years as an educational researcher and educational policy analyst. I hope that sharing them with you will be of interest.

—David Berliner
Oakland, CA
May, 2025

A Hug for Jennifer

I met Jennifer for the first time at a party. She taught elementary school to mostly white, middle-class kids in a suburb of San Francisco. We chatted about education for a while, and she invited me to visit her class. I like visiting classes, in part because they are always so difficult to understand. It is an enormous challenge to witness and make sense of the interaction of *teachers* and *students* with *curriculum materials* in a *classroom setting*. Sometimes, with teachers you come to admire, it is like trying to put together a recipe after tasting a delicious dish. It's hard to figure out the ingredients that made it so special.

More frequently, my observations struck me as a bit like trying to study what comes out the end of a funnel without much confidence that you know all about what went into the funnel. It's hard to figure out the ingredients, the stuff that makes a classroom hum or fail. Some of the things that are sure to have entered the funnel are: all of society's values; the pop culture of the day, particularly as represented on television, YouTube, and TikTok; the individual child rearing practices of 25 or so different families; the economic, physical, and mental health of the people in the neighborhood around the school; the teaching skills, content knowledge, prejudices, and personal family concerns of the individual teacher; the leadership skills of the principal; the educational directives issued by the school district and the state; the support or anger of the schools' parents and districts' school board, and even more. After the large, open end of the funnel receives a thousand items of this type, I wander into a classroom to observe a teacher attempting to create something sensible and unique out of whatever comes tumbling out the small end of the funnel. You really never know what you'll see and hear when you go to observe a classroom.

Besides being challenged to unravel what goes on in such complex environments, I also visit classes regularly for another reason. I do it because of my profound distaste for the many people who freely comment about education, but spend no significant amounts of time visiting schools and classes. These education bashers regularly provide the media with false descriptions of America's schools, inadequate critiques of the education system, and impractical suggestions for school improvement. For example, President Donald Trump (2000) said, "According to school-testing experts' rule of thumb, the average child's achievement score *declines* about 1 percent for each year they're in school. That gives the expression dumbing down a whole new meaning. Schools may be hazardous to your child's intellectual health."

So I took Jennifer up on her offer and I began to drop in on her class occasionally, since her school was on the way to my work. On one of those visits, I learned a lesson about teachers and observing in classrooms that affected the rest of my career.

Jennifer taught 4th grade. She obviously had self-confidence because she invited me to drop in any time, unannounced, to observe her class. I timed one of these visits so I could avoid the taking of attendance, the principal's announcements, and other morning housekeeping activities. As I had planned, I arrived just as a reading session was about to start. From the seating chart Jennifer had given me, I soon identified Alec. He had caught my eye, though I was not yet sure why. Alec sat at the side of the class, his face a blank—impassive, masklike. I felt compelled to watch him repeatedly throughout the reading period. Despite the generally upbeat lesson the class was enjoying, Alec displayed no emotions. He seemed barely to follow what was going on around him. I was surprised that Jennifer, who usually was so equitable in her interactions with the children, seemed to be ignoring Alec. When reading was finished and the children went out for recess, Alec remained in the class, the same blank look on his face, and with Jennifer still showing the same pleasant but unconcerned manner.

When the children returned from their break, no one talked to Alec. From my perspective, his teacher and his classmates acted like Alec did not exist. To me, the outside observer, it looked like a modern version of an old punishment: Alec was being shunned! I was losing my curiosity about what was happening and, instead, began to get angry at Jennifer and the other children.

Mathematics work began and Jennifer called small groups of children to the desk where she presented some new concepts, while most of the rest of the class did problems in their workbooks. Alec did nothing. He never took out his workbook and Jennifer never criticized him, and she never invited him to the desk, as she did the other students. I could not stop myself from focusing on this situation, to the exclusion of whatever else was happening in the class. I grieved for this child, remembering my worst days as a schoolboy and my terror of being ostracized, even for a short time. I remembered the games we sometimes played, games in which we were so cruel to one another. My memory filled suddenly with an event from junior high school. A time when we once had "Don't talk to Bobby day!," a day when my classmates and I purposely set out to hurt another child. But never had I seen a teacher join in, which seemed to be what I was watching. As my fantasies about Alec's plight merged with my own resurrected childhood fears and embarrassment, I began to get angrier and angrier at Jennifer.

When the lunch bell finally rang, and the children filed out with Alec, still alone among them, I approached Jennifer's desk. I tried to keep the anger I felt under control. I pushed away, to the farthest reaches of my mind, the shame and the embarrassment I felt about being both perpetrator and victim of such exclusionary practices in the past. I said to Jennifer, in as controlled a manner as possible, that Alec did not seem to be participating much in classroom activities.

When Jennifer responded, I learned a lesson about the importance of understanding the intentions, thoughts, feelings, and beliefs of the persons we as researchers intend to study. It is difficult, of course, in any communication setting, to genuinely understand another person's thoughts and feelings. But when you observe as a social scientist, rather than an ordinary person chatting with others, this commonplace problem in interpersonal communication looms much larger. A lack of understanding, or a misunderstanding of another person's intentions, can lead a social scientist to make dangerously flawed inferences about other persons' behaviors.

Jennifer explained. Alec's brother had been shot and killed by the police the night before—a rarity in the middle-class neighborhood that the school served. And it happened at home, in front of Alec. Before I arrived that morning, Jennifer had taken Alec aside and told him how sorry she was for his whole family. She thought the day might be a tough one for him, so she told Alec that he should feel free to participate or not, to do whatever he felt like. She would let him decide how he wanted to use his time. She also told him how glad they all were that he was in the class and when he felt like getting involved with everything again to just start doing so. The other students had all heard about what had happened and were not shunning Alec, but rather giving him some breathing room. My anger, of course, was gone. In its place was a sense of wonder.

How many incidents like this one did Jennifer have to deal with in a typical week or month, on top of her academic responsibilities? Who taught her to confront this awful event in such a straightforward and caring manner? Actually, I am still not sure it was the best response to Alec's loss and sadness, but to me, it sure seemed to be a sensible response. Did she have such sensitivity to youngsters when she first started teaching, or is this part of what teachers learn as they gain experience? How could I have been so blind as to what was going on that I grew angry at Jennifer? How many other times have I observed classes and reached completely wrong conclusions about what was going on?

After this incident, when I was working in classrooms, I was sure that I had become a better social scientist. I tried always to understand the intentions of the teachers that I studied. I spent time with them, trying to learn what they were going to teach, what special constraints they were under, and what they thought I should know before I began watching them. When I did this, I was sure that my conclusions about what occurred in their classrooms were different than before I had met Jennifer. More importantly, however, is that my views about observation in classrooms changed. I once thought that some kind of "raw" observation was possible, that a kind of neutral, objective mirror of classroom life could be obtained. But Jennifer taught me that is just not true.

Observations can be *relatively* pure, *relatively* objective, but never completely so. In fact, it is likely that observations and interpretations of classroom life without understanding teachers and their intentions are likely to be more distorted than observations and interpretations made with such knowledge. I believe this despite the obvious loss of objectivity and neutrality that must occur as teachers and researchers get to know each other better. I'll say it clearly: Interpretations of a teacher's behavior without knowledge of the teacher's intentions are either useless or, worse, inaccurate and unjust. My visit to Jennifer's classroom that particular day as an outsider led me to inaccurate and unjust conclusions about what was going on. It was sobering.

There is also a bigger issue to which this incident is relevant. Since we cannot adequately interpret life in classrooms unless we have an insider's understanding of that classroom, how is it possible for principals, department heads, and others who evaluate teachers to do so when they visit a teacher's classroom infrequently, stay for the briefest period of time, and distance themselves from the teacher to maintain objectivity? The unbiased observations of the outsider may be a requirement in physics, chemistry, oncology, and other natural and biological sciences. Doing "good science" certainly requires the illusion of total objectivity, even though the best of scientists acknowledge that such a goal is impossible to achieve. But in areas of social behavior and especially those research areas concerned with classrooms and schools, such calls for objectivity are probably misplaced. Perhaps the only way to understand life in classrooms is to visit frequently, stay for a lengthy period of time, and share the teacher's vision of what is intended. Evaluations of teachers that rely too heavily on formal observation instruments, notions of objectivity, and the outsider's view of the classroom are likely to report, as I might have, that Jennifer was an insensitive, uncaring human being. A more appropriate evaluation system would have caused the observer to hug Jennifer and give thanks that she chose to teach children.

Teachers Teach
It's What They Do!

A few years ago, I lost my wife. The Alzheimer's disease she was diagnosed with kept getting worse, eventually disrupting the wonderful life we led together over many decades.

Over the last few years, I took care of her as best I could. But eventually I had to place her into a memory care unit, where she now resides, and has round-the-clock care. I took an apartment in the same building, and I see her almost every day. She usually knows who I am, but once in a while, her eyes have a certain empty quality when I appear, and then I am not completely sure she really does know me. Like many with loved ones who have some form of dementia, it is both a repetitive and yet always shocking experience to be seen as a stranger by your loved one. I remember vividly the first time I experienced such a shock. We were sitting outdoors on a patio, on a beautiful evening in Sedona, Arizona, surrounded by red rock mountains, listening to folk and popular music played by a trio of our neighbors. My wife turned to me and smiled, and I saw, for the first time, that blank quality in her eyes which, sadly, is now evident more frequently. I asked if she was okay. She said yes. And then, after 40 years of being together, I asked the oddest question. For some reason I asked her if she knew who I was. She said, "No, but you seem like a nice man!" That was the evening that I knew I had lost my wife.

Now and again my wife comes back to me, but, sadly, this happens less and less frequently. What amazes me, however, is that certain endearing qualities of hers have not disappeared. She was a mother, a public school teacher, and a principal before becoming a professor—and there are times when those previous roles are quite evident. For example, she still frequently teaches children and tells their parents what to do and how they might do it!

How, you may ask, can an Alzheimer's patient do that while locked in a memory care facility? Easy! She sees and talks to kids and their parents that you and I cannot see. If my wife were in New England in the 1600s, I am sure that she would have been burned at the stake for regularly consorting with spirits. But in her confused mind, she is talking to such "spirits" pretty regularly, and she does so in her role as "teacher."

For example, she often stands at her window, overlooking a busy street, and lectures the children she sees outside—children you and I can neither see nor hear. This morning she was telling one child that she needed to read more. That reading was much more important and better for her than playing in the street. To another, she was reciting the dangers of playing in the median with all the cars speeding by, and she chastised the child's (invisible) mother for allowing such dangerous play. My wife regularly informed the mothers she talks with that they had obligations to keep their children safe and they also needed to read to them, limit television, and see that they had good medical care and nutritious food to eat.

On another day, to another child that she alone could see and talk with, she gave a mini-lecture on why children needed to sleep more and eat food that will help them grow, and also why they needed to listen to their mothers. To another unseen mother, she talked about why she should read to her little girl—how good that was for the child's growth. On still another day, she was helping a child with her schoolwork. On yet another of my visits, she was giving advice to a girl with hurt feelings, informing her about how to get along with others—especially the mean ones, of which there are always a few.

These are ordinarily not 1-minute conversations, but more like mini-lectures, and frequently of substantial duration. They include laughter, because my wife, like almost all elementary school teachers, delights in the things their young students say and do. And just as she lectures the children and their mothers, she also vocalizes their responses to her commentaries. So I am privy to the complete conversation between my wife and an assortment of people whom I cannot see or hear. As I listen in to both sides of these conversations, I am so happy that my wife is their teacher. She is their counselor. She is their advisor.

I have lost my wife. But the world has not lost the contributions of a wonderful teacher. Teachers teach. It's what they do. It's just too bad that this latest batch of students and their parents are unable to tell my wife how much they appreciate her guidance.

Interest, Not Just IQ, Buildeth the Mind!

We know children have short attention spans. That seems to be common knowledge. But of course, it's not true. Have you ever watched a 10-year-old spend 3 hours learning a video game or building with LEGO bricks? Did you ever see a 7-year-old child with a magnet or a magnifying glass, playing with it for an uninterrupted hour or more? Can you remember ever being that kid?

The fact is, we all have shown short attention spans in dealing with certain issues and topics that we face in our lives. The common element, for both kids and adults, are issues, topics, and tasks in which we have no interest. Attention span is not a property of kids or adults, like height or weight, but it is a property of their interaction with particular tasks.

We also "know" that children don't have fully developed cognitive skills, so complex concepts are a bit beyond them. Perspective-taking, in-depth understanding of complex and abstract concepts, and fully operational thought is really only possible, say some psychologists, after they reach adolescence. Neuropsychologists have added their two cents, informing us that youth must have fully developed frontal lobes to be "good thinkers," and maturity of that kind may not occur until around 20 years of age. But of course, all this is nonsense as well.

Young dinosaur enthusiasts, Civil War buffs, and railroad enthusiasts have been found by researchers to think better, more clearly, and more deeply about issues relating to dinosaurs, the Civil War, and trains than college students who did not have backgrounds in such areas (Chi & Koeske, 1983). Sadly, a good deal of 20th-century psychology has been about *under*estimating the abilities of infants and youth. The famous Swiss psychologist Jean Piaget probably set child psychology back decades as he convinced everyone that youth cannot competently reason until well into their teens. In fact, in the past few decades we have learned that motivated study can make an expert out of almost anyone. A normal mind, coupled with both the will and the time to practice, that puts in lots of *deliberate practice* can build our expertise in almost any field—chess, knowledge of dinosaurs, the Civil War, railroad engines, and so forth (Ericsson, 1996). So why don't most children strive to be great scientists, mathematicians, writers, and so forth?

The answer may be found in my observations of a child learning the rules for the card game *Magic: The Gathering*. The child was Mackenzie the Magnificent—my grandson. When not being magnificent, he was actually a normal, everyday 11-year-old kid learning to play that card game with me observing him. Here is some of the background for the game of *Magic* (Wizards of the Coast, n.d.).

> In *Magic: The Gathering*, a Planeswalker is a powerful mage [magician] who is able to travel across the planes of existence. There are infinite worlds across the Multiverse, and Planeswalkers are unique in their ability to move from one world to the next, expanding their knowledge and power through the experiences they collect there.
>
> *The Spark: One in a Million.* One in a million sentient beings are born with "the spark," the ineffable essence that makes an individual capable of becoming a Planeswalker. Of those born with "the spark," even fewer "ignite" their spark, enabling them to realize their potential and travel the planes. Most Planeswalkers have their spark ignited as the result of a great crisis or trauma, but every awakening is different. A near-death experience might ignite a Planeswalker's spark, but so could a sudden, life-changing epiphany or a meditative trance that enables the mage's grasp of some transcendent truth. There are as many such stories as there are Planeswalkers.
>
> *The Blind Eternities.* The "Blind Eternities" is a poetic term for the space between planes. The Blind Eternities are a chaotic, logic-defying place of quasi-existence filled with raw potential called Æther. Only Planeswalkers can survive there, and only for a limited time. Mortal beings without the Planeswalker spark are soon destroyed by raw entropy and uncontained mania that suffuses the Blind Eternities.

There is more to learn about the game of *Magic* (see below). What I have presented thus far was just to impress those who do not know the game with how remarkably complex it is. I think its 243 pages of definitions and rules make Bridge look like a game for those of limited cognitive capacity (Magic: The Gathering, n.d.)! *Magic* is one of hundreds of games, some computerized, some not, that I could have chosen to illustrate this important point: *There are few limits on what youth can know and do if they are motivated.* Interest, not just IQ, buildeth the mind!

I chose *Magic* to illustrate this point because I spent many hours at the game store watching my grandson and others around his same age learn it. They were, by the way, under the tutelage of and enthralled by a "grand master." He was a kid who was around 14 years old!

I have given a lot of thought to those few days of observation. I saw feats of memory and mastery of strategies by young children that I believed to be extraordinary. I thought about the intrinsic interest that such a game has for the young. I thought also about the level of cognitive ability necessary to become good at the game. I concluded, sadly, that I was not smart enough to ever play it well, but I also concluded that a lot of the people who build our nation's curricula must dislike kids. I reached that conclusion because so little in the typical school curriculum has the appeal that *Magic* had for the kids that I watched.

To me, *Magic* looked like play for gifted adults, but just happens to be played instead by children and adolescents of apparently ordinary brainpower. I also thought that many of the kids who were playing quite adequately were likely to be considered incompetent by adults who know nothing about the games played by these same youth. That is because too often the competencies of our youth are judged in settings that hold no great interest to them. And so, too often, older generations think of younger generations as deficient in their cognitive abilities. Ask our business leaders and our politicians; they almost all have something negative to say about the competency of our youth, forgetting what their grandparents said about their generation!

As I watched the game unfold, I thought also about the vocabulary needed to understand the game. I thought of the memorization needed to learn the "powers" possessed by different cards. But these new words and complex rules were learned in a meaningful context, and that surely makes a difference. The words to be learned were not isolated on lists to be memorized, as we sometimes see in contemporary classrooms. The sounds of words were not learned by mastering nonsense syllables and nonwords, as in some phonics programs used throughout our nation. In *Magic*, real words and their sounds were learned in a meaningful context, and none of the kids I observed seemed to have problems doing so. Watching the kids learn *Magic* made me worry that too much classroom time might be spent on the mindless drilling of vocabulary and the sounds of words, when such things can be learned so much more easily, quickly and permanently when the words to be learned are functional for the learner. The excerpt that follows gives a very complex overview of the game of *Magic*, which the young children I observed read and worked on comprehending.

*   *   *

Mages and Planeswalkers of the Multiverse can cast a vast array of spells— they can drain the life of a foe, supplement their allies with arcane strength, even summon a dragon. But all magic requires mana. Mana is the magical energy that powers spells. Where do you get it? Mana comes from the land. Mages must know a place to gather mana from it. Mana is scarce, so mages don't have infinite energy to cast spells. They must make bonds with lands to gain new sources of mana.

There are five colors of mana, and each comes from a different type of land:

White—Plains
Blue—Islands
Black—Swamps
Red—Mountains
Green—Forests

Each color is driven by different values (see Table 3.1).

So, dear reader, have you got all that? Can you follow the rules? You see, there are these creatures, Planeswalkers, in *two* states—those with sparks and those without. They cross the blind eternities, between planes, and use magic there. That requires mana of *five* different kinds, obtained in five lands. But the mana has *three* different characteristics. So, I think, at a minimum, this makes for at least 30 distinct kinds of adventures ($2 \times 5 \times 3$), if I got it right. And I am not at all sure I do have it right!

As I watched and listened, I thought it odd that many kids who were, perhaps, "slow" in school were easily coping with the complex concepts, and were learning clever strategies as they learned to play this complex game. The grand master I talked to later agreed. He told me that many kids who were having academic trouble turn out to be great *Magic* players!

What can explain that? Perhaps an explanation is in "competency motivation"—the need to master things *of interest*. Educational psychologists like me have studied the drive to competency, the desire for mastery. And that leads many of us to believe that somehow, in school settings, for too many kids, the motivational systems that lead to success are not being engaged. We should worry about that because when competency motivation is engaged, the difficulty in learning all sorts of tasks is overcome—as with the kids I watched learning *Magic*.

At first, I felt a little bit inadequate watching Mackenzie and his agemates learn this stuff quickly while I was unable to do so. But I think I know why. I really didn't give a damn! I had nothing but the most minimum passing interest in MAGIC. Somehow with my bigger brain, my fully and well-developed frontal lobes, my wealth of life experience, and my Stanford

Table 3.1. Characteristics Associated With Each Color in the Game of Magic

WHITE	BLUE	BLACK	RED	GREEN
Order	Knowledge	Darkness	Freedom	Growth
Protection	Manipulation	Ambition	Emotion	Instinct
Light	Illusion	Death	Impulse	Nature

PhD, I was unable to keep all the rules and strategies straight. Conclusion? Interest, not just IQ, buildeth the mind!

In fact, as time went on and I learned more, the game got even more complex, and yet it continued to hold the interest of the kids. Kids like these will spend hours reading, discussing, and arguing about the rules, strategies, and events that make up *Magic*. By comparison, regular school lessons must appear dull and boring. But is it also possible that school tasks were also not nearly as cognitively taxing?

Furthermore, after classroom instruction, students often face multiple-choice items to assess what they have learned instead of allowing them to demonstrate their competency through their performance, as they do when playing *Magic* or a hundred other similar games. Shouldn't we try to find ways of showing acquired competency other than through multiple-choice assessments? For example, by writing and performing plays, making presentations to community members, engaging in debates, writing letters to editors, and dozens of other ways that creative democratic educators, like Debbie Meier (Meier & Knoester, 2017; see also Au & Tempel, 2012) have used in schools for years would fit the bill.

I worry that too many business leaders and politicians have too often denied their own common sense and the extant research on motivation. And in doing that, they have forced schools to get even better at what they were already pretty good at—boring students to death!

Is it possible that the boring schools of my generation are even more boring than ever before, as a function of the Common Core curriculum and associated standardized achievement tests? Could the dullest of the teachers who taught my generation now be even worse? Even some of the most engaging teachers of an earlier era frequently complain to me that they have lost their spark trying to fulfill expectations that test scores, derived from mostly multiple-choice items, keep rising. Too many teachers say they have abandoned art, music, sports, social studies, drama, visiting hospitals, taking field biology trips, and so forth, so they can drill their students on the tests required by federal and state laws (Nichols & Berliner, 2007). This is terrible educational policy! How will our children ever become fascinated by learning all about bugs, birds, trees, airports, and the like without field trips? Where will our youth get their ideas about the complex world we live in without vists to municipal gardens, hospitals, art museums, county courts, and waste disposal and water purification plants, or from vists to a hundred other places of beauty and/or interest? Something important may be lost if field trips are curtailed or abandoned to prepare for tests, as seems to be the case. Has anyone ever traced the numbers of physicians, nurses, firefighters, artists, and pilots we have because of school trips to hospitals, fire stations, art museums, and airports?

This all leads me to believe that too many businesspeople and politicians who support the test-based accountability system of contemporary

American education, with its relentless pressure to narrow the curriculum and to drill kids on the material that gets made into test items, are denying their own youth. They deny their own experience as parents, workers, and employers. They deny their common sense and the extant research on motivation. Their misunderstanding and inflexibility about how to help children learn is hurting our nation. They need to be told over and over that school dropouts are not always those who have trouble with an academic curriculum. In fact, the Gates Foundation estimates that close to 50% of America's dropouts are quite able to handle the curriculum, *but are bored out of their minds* (Bridgeland et al., 2006)*!*

No one I know in education expects that a curriculum can be all fun. But a test-focused education system has stopped many teachers from engaging in activities that can pique youths' interest. And yet, here is the irony! So many of the businesspeople and politicians who seem to yell a lot and the loudest about the fact that we are not producing enough engineers and computer scientists have picked the wrong school policies to produce those individuals! Those businesspeople and politicians, from Bill Gates to Barack Obama, who worry that China or India will surpass us in technology, or who scold us because our very survival as a nation depends on scientists and mathematicians, have picked the absolutely wrong policies to develop such people. You see, the research tells us that enrollments in science, technology, engineering, and mathematics fields are less related to ability than they are to simple interest. In our nation, in our culture, it's not always the very brightest who go into such fields, it's more frequently the most interested! So if we don't teach these subjects in ways that pique the interest of our youth, we'll never get as many of our youth, especially the brightest of them, into these fields.

Despite the folklore, math and physics, or engineering and computer science, are not "hard" subjects to master if students are as interested in them as the kids I observed were in learning *Magic*. Our kids need to be motivated to take some of the subjects that require many hours of study, such as engineering, mathematics, and science. But they will never be motivated in the numbers that our nation needs if their schooling is more dependent on drill and practice and makes less use of project-based and problem-based education. Our students need real projects and interesting problems to solve; they need apprenticeships in laboratories with working scientists; they need some inquiry-based instruction so that their sense of wonder and imagination is piqued—as happens when they learn some computer games, and as I witnessed when they were learning *Magic*.

The situation is even worse among the children of poorer Americans. These are the children who frequently attend schools labeled "D" or "F," a rating based on demographics, not necessarily the quality of instruction. The students in these schools are the ones most likely to be drilled in preparation for tests, and their teachers are the most likely to be told they might be fired if scores in math and science do not rise. But it is much more likely that interest, not drill, will buildeth the mind and, as a consequence, improveth the test score!

Enough! It is time to rethink what we are doing. Einstein said it best: "A society's competitive advantage will come not from how well its schools teach the multiplication and periodic tables, but from how well they stimulate imagination and creativity." Our youth need to play more games like MAGIC and spend less time on curriculum that resembles Trivial Pursuit!

Public Education and the Health of Our Nation's Democracy*

I once put a question to an informant I thought to be both well read and nonideological. I asked, "What is the link between public education and democracy?" My informant responded with the following:

> Public education and democracy are closely linked, as education plays a critical role in the functioning of democratic societies. In a democratic society, citizens are expected to participate in the political process, make informed decisions, and hold elected officials accountable. This requires a certain level of education and knowledge about the political process and government institutions.
>
> Public education helps ensure that all citizens have equal access to the knowledge and skills they need to participate fully in democratic life. By providing education to all children, regardless of their social or economic background, public education helps level the playing field and reduces inequality. It also helps promote a common understanding of democratic values and principles, such as freedom of speech, equality, and justice.
>
> Furthermore, public education helps foster critical thinking, independent thinking, and creativity, all of which are essential for a vibrant and healthy democracy. It provides opportunities for students to learn about different perspectives and to engage in respectful dialogue and debate. This helps build a more informed and engaged citizenry, which is crucial for the functioning of a democratic society.
>
> In conclusion, public education is an essential component of democracy, as it helps to ensure that all citizens have the knowledge and skills they need to participate fully in the political process and to make informed decisions. It also helps promote equality, foster critical thinking, and build a more informed and engaged citizenry.

My informant, however, was not a human. I asked my question of the artificially intelligent chatbot ChatGPT (Open AI, 2022). My own beliefs are quite

---

*A version of this essay first appeared in a special issue of the journal *Educational Policy Analysis Archive*, Vol. 31 (2023) (see https://doi.org/10.14507/epaa.31.8061)

compatible with the chatbot, and I found that to be good news. That is because, after its digestion of millions of documents about democracy and education, ChatGPT expressed the kinds of beliefs that are widely shared by Americans. These are what might easily be called "mainstream beliefs," and they are consistent with the views of many scholars (Berliner & Hermanns, 2021).

ChatGPT, however, seemed unable to recognize that not everyone wants the nation's schools to be public and many citizens hold negative views of our public system. For instance, many charter, voucher, and religious school supporters, and parents who home school their children, might find much to argue about with the answer provided by ChatGPT. My views about our public schools and their role in our democracy follow.

LEARNING FOR EMPLOYABILITY VS. LEARNING FOR LIFE

ChatGPT seemed unconcerned about the economic role expected of public schools in American society. Many of our citizens, and over many decades, believe that "preparation for employment" should be the major focus of our schools, but "job preparation" is much too narrow a role for education in a democracy. The "schooling for employability" argument almost always requires narrowing the curriculum to fit economic purposes. The curriculum recommendations we might get, then, are that schools teach "how to type" (50 years ago), or "to code" (in more recent times). Learning such skills is easily defended. But with limited time for educating our youth, isn't our nation, ultimately, better served by encouraging critical thinking about history, government, civics, political science, and social studies, in addition to or as a substitute for focusing on employment-oriented skills? I certainly think so, particularly given the quick changes in the skills needed for employability that occur in a modern economy.

Preparation for life in a democratic society requires a broader conception of the school curriculum than preparation for employment. For example, in 2022, only 30–40% of eligible voters cast votes in some states, while in other states over 60% of eligible citizens voted (Ballotpedia, 2023). Neither statistic is heartening and may be linked to a failure of America's public educational system to prepare our youth for the obligations of citizenship. Such data brings to mind the warning that Benjamin Franklin gave to Americans, namely, that he and the founding fathers created a republic—*but only if we can keep it*! (McHenry, 1787).

CURRICULAR CHOICE AND DEMOCRATIC LIVING

Training for democracy requires a commitment by our schools to strongly value students' freedom, *empowering* them, to the extent possible, to choose their future. In my belief system, greatly influenced by John Dewey, democratic schools should promote the talents and preferences expressed by their students and be less swayed by the desires of industry or the Department of Labor's annual report on the best-paying jobs of the future. My "apprenticeship" view of democracy grants youth *a modicum* of freedom, and would accommodate to *at least some* of their desires.

Federal programs such as No Child Left Behind, Race for the Top, and the Every Child Succeeds Act did not foster students' (nor teachers') ability to make many choices for themselves. Ignoring our students' freedom to make at least some decisions about their learning is to blithely prepare students for a life strongly prescribed and proscribed by others, aiding more in their preparation for life in an autocratic, dictatorial, or even tyrannical society. So I would like all U.S. students to be considered apprentices in our democracy, and that requires some changes to schooling as we know it.

*   *   *

Even a small degree of freedom to suggest and choose at least some of their educational experiences provides such an apprenticeship. And it seems not to have deleterious effects. For example, "The Eight-Year Study" (Aiken, 1942) is nearly 100 years old, and because of that it is often ignored. But from 1930 to 1942, researchers studied hundreds of students in 30 unique "progressive" high schools. Participating high schools agreed to use a nonstandard curriculum. Students were required to study some of their state's basic curricula. However, they also received credit for choosing to study, think, write about, and build almost anything they wanted by taking other courses. Students were encouraged to engage in highly unusual, self-determined projects and papers, few of which would have been approved had they been subject to the standard high school curriculum of their time.

There were 1,475 students attending these progressive schools, studying a *nonstandard* high school curriculum. They went on to about 300 colleges and universities (Lipka et al., 1998, p. 130). Each progressive school graduate was matched with a traditional school graduate with similar background characteristics as a control. Researchers continued to monitor and document student progress and achievements as they graduated high school. Many educators thought it would be difficult for these students to compete in college, as they did not study the standard, state-sanctioned curriculum. Therefore, the universities were also asked to monitor for deficits, since the students had not been "properly prepared" for college.

Regardless of the college attended, analyses showed that the progressive school graduates showed more leadership; joined and led more clubs; were rated as thinking more clearly; had a greater interest in books, music, and art; got slightly better grades; and won more academic honors (e.g., Phi

Beta Kappa and honor roll designations) than did students from traditional schools. And they *demonstrated a better understanding of democracy.*

A sub-study of graduates from the six most progressive schools—what traditionalists considered the "wildest" schools—revealed that these students not only scored well above traditionally educated students, but they even surpassed their peers from other progressive schools! They were also rated the highest in intellectual drive, thinking ability, and participation in extracurricular activity. What more could a democracy ask for from the students it educates, students who will soon be adult citizens registering to vote?

The scholars concluded that the widespread belief that students must have a prescribed school curriculum *is not tenable.* Instead, they said that studying almost anything broadly and in-depth, with some (but not necessarily a lot of) teacher support, prepares youth for the highest levels of scholarship. Apparently there were no negative effects from studying "this" instead of "that" *if it was studied well.*

The lesson *not* learned from this research is that learning seriously and deeply, and sharing that knowledge with one's peers, parents, and the school faculty via various platforms (e.g., papers, PowerPoint, YouTube, film, television, music, art, etc.), presents a viable alternative to learning only the required state or district curriculum. In other words, self-chosen educational experiences bestow apprenticeship-based learning opportunities unavailable through mandated curricula.

IN SCHOOLS THAT PRACTICE DEMOCRACY, DEMOCRACY MIGHT BE LEARNED

Regardless of how students engage with the curriculum, it is highly unlikely that apprenticeship-based learning will occur if school systems are not run democratically. Noted educator and school principal Debbie Meier (2021) asks:

> Can a school divided by class and race, built around authoritarian principles, reasonably be expected to "train" or educate the future citizens of our state in the workings of democracy? If democracy were really such a great idea—one we claim to go to war to save—how come our public schools are anything but? In fact, I'd argue that America's schools, on average, represent one of the most authoritarian institutions in society. (p. 163)

Meier notes that schools best *serve* democracy by *being* democracies. They must be designed and operated for the people, by the people. To achieve something close to actual democratic schooling, Meier believes that each school should have its own school board. She argues that local schools cannot be considered democratically run if they are not *independently* designing educational experiences and debating educational issues. She posits that local school board members should include teachers, parents, students, and community representatives. Each local school board would link to the district's board because that is where centralized administrative decisions are made, especially fiscal ones.

Further, a democratically run school should also pick its principal, or at a minimum, its lead educator, and not be assigned one by a centralized board. How can a school be called a democratic workplace if those who work there do not have a vote on who leads them? Meier also notes, sadly, that students attending almost all public, private, and charter schools read about, but rarely have personal experience with, schools that are democratically run. This common state of affairs limits students from serving any sort of an apprenticeship in democracy.

ASSESSMENT PRACTICES AND CONFLICTS WITH DEMOCRATIC LEARNING

In the last few decades, more schools and districts have become less democratic due to concerns about America's allegedly low achievement, as demonstrated by standardized test scores. There is considerable evidence that the nation has panicked over state, national, and international assessment scores. The knee-jerk reaction to purportedly low scores has been to teach to the test, leading to a narrowing of each state's curriculum. Thus, in trying to raise test scores, America's leaders have often undermined democratic processes in school after school (Davis, 2010).

For example, before Congress passed the No Child Left Behind Act of 2001, social studies in elementary schools were taught an average of 239 minutes a week. After nationwide testing mandates were enacted, class time in social studies decreased to 164 minutes a week, for a loss of 76 minutes a week. This was a 32% drop in coursework in subjects such as geography, economics, culture, history, political science, and government. Additionally, coursework in art and music was reduced by 35% and physical education was reduced by 35% as schools dedicated more time to meeting testing goals (Center on Education Policy, 2008, p. 4; see also Educating for American Democracy Initiative, 2021). In a test-oriented culture, what gets tested is what gets taught. Thus, courses on government, civics, and history have lost out to courses that might improve test scores in reading and mathematics.

Mandated testing has propagated a nationwide attitude of "success by any means." The Atlanta Public School system in Atlanta, Georgia, is a prime example of what happens when test results take precedence over concerns for learning (Vogell, 2011). School leaders were discovered to have either changed test scores or forced teachers to do so. Democracy, professionalism, and empathy for students fled our public schools as teachers were forced to cheat to protect their jobs. An 800-page report on the Atlanta cheating scandal (Martel, 2011) documents the "culture of fear, intimidation, and retaliation" teachers face in schools nationwide, where test scores are prioritized and democratic processes ignored. Under such high-pressure conditions, abusive administrative behavior became common, undermining desires for democratic school environments for teachers and their students.

In systems of education where test scores matter most, we frequently hear disturbing statements from educators. For example, one Colorado elementary school teacher noted that ". . . We don't take as many field trips. We don't do community outreach like we used to, like visiting the nursing home or cleaning up the park because we had adopted a park, and that was our job, to keep it clean. Well, we don't have time for that anymore" (Taylor et al., 2003, p. 30). Another Colorado teacher says, "We only teach to the test even at 2nd grade and have stopped teaching science and social studies" (Taylor et al., 2003, p. 31). These examples are 2 decades old, but no different from the conversations I have with contemporary administrators and teachers who are also subject to testing pressures.

RESTRICTING FREEDOM OF INFORMATION: COMPROMISING A RIGHT OF INDIVIDUALS IN A DEMOCRATIC NATION

In many autocratic nations, books, television shows, radio broadcasts, newspapers, and social media are censored, and those espousing democratic ideas are banned. This practice is meant to keep citizens unaware of what is happening in their nation, and perhaps preventing them from rebelling against those in power. Authoritarian governments and dictatorships try to control information, but censorship also may have its roots in racial hatred, efforts to maintain economic power, or the promotion of religious domination. Thus, it is quite concerning to learn who, and what ideology, is behind the recent alarming increase in banning books in U.S. public school libraries.

According to a recent report (Friedman & Johnson, 2022), 1,648 unique book titles by 1,261 authors have been banned in 138 school districts in 32 states. At that time, Texas led the nation with 751–1,000 bans, followed by Florida (501–750), then Tennessee and New York (251–500). Twenty-eight other states have banned 50 or fewer books. The most censored books deal with LGBTQ+ subject matter (41%), and those that deal with race and racism (40%) whose primary characters are non-white. Notably, 161, or 10%, of banned books dealt with rights and activism. Censorship limits youths' access to a wide range of perspectives and ideas (Friedman & Johnson, 2022). Moreover, it reinforces racism and prejudices and undermines two key tenets of U.S. democracy—freedom of information and of speech. Therefore, censorship is not merely *un*democratic; it is *anti*democratic.

Members of democratic societies need access to trustworthy news representing a vast array of themes, ideas, and perspectives. This array must include views that may be offensive, even repugnant, for many people, such as books that support antidemocratic ideals (e.g., *Mein Kampf*, *The Protocols of the Elders of Zion*, *The Communist Manifesto*, and books on the Ku Klux Klan). Yet, we need these books to understand how human society has evolved. Banning books like these because they are "dangerous," or "subversive," ensures ignorance about our world, and that is not healthy for furthering a democracy.

I must confess that one of the proudest days I ever had as a professor/scholar/author was when I joined the elite in the humanities and sciences. Two of my writings were banned in my home state of Arizona! *The Manufactured Crisis* (Berliner & Biddle, 1995) and a chapter titled "If the Underlying Premise for No Child Left Behind Is False, How Can That Act Solve Our Problems?" The chapter appeared in a book edited by Ken Goodman and others with the subversive title *Saving Our Schools* (Goodman et al., 2004). My dangerous ideas were right up there with other authors whose books were banned on that same day, including books by James Baldwin (*The Fire Next Time*), William Shakespeare (*The Tempest*), Henry David Thoreau (*Civil Disobedience*), Jonathan Kozol (*Savage Inequalities*), and bell hooks (*Feminism Is for Everybody: Passionate Politics*).

Numerous activist groups with religious or political agendas, and even government officials, have pushed for book bans (Friedman & Johnson, 2022). But minority youth, be they Jewish, Black, Muslim, queer, trans, or other youth, need to see themselves in the books they read to understand where they fit in the world. Other book banners claim they are acting as patriots. However, they are more likely to be hiding the fact that they want to keep youth and the public ignorant of the vast literature on alternatives to capitalist America. For example, Northern European nations are quite content with their various forms of socialism. Moreover, in those nations, democracy and socialism are strongly linked together. These alternatives to capitalist America are described and evaluated in the books and magazines that reside in school and public libraries across the nation. This makes many Americans nervous. The Daily Kos (2022), commenting on the current book banning, said:

> This was never about keeping kids "safe," but has always been about keeping people uneducated and ignorant. Suppressing diverse ideas has always been the hallmark of conservatism, and free libraries stand in the way of their goal. Libraries help people who need it most, which, according to a right-wing billionaire, is the worst possible use of resources. Libraries serve their community without regard for profit, which is antithetical to the capitalist mindset that their wealthy de-funders have. Yet education and easy access to information are the greatest threats to the conservative movement and to the protection of their ill-gotten wealth. Of course, they are attacking libraries—and schools. (para. 13)

Youth do not need censors. They need access, but also parents, educators, librarians, and school counselors who are knowledgeable and supportive. To provide youth with many of these resources requires the expenditure of public funds. And collecting tax money for paying such professionals is much more difficult than pushing to ban books and squelching free thinking.

Keeping our libraries open and our librarians both well trained and well paid is a necessity for a healthy democracy. Librarians are experts with the knowledge to advise students and citizens alike about books and other educative resources to satisfy their curiosity and research interests. As Franklin Roosevelt said in a letter to a book publisher, "I have an unshaken conviction that democracy can never be undermined if we maintain our library resources and a national intelligence capable of utilizing them" (Daily Kos, 2022, epigraph). Roosevelt seems to be saying something about reciprocity: Good schools need good libraries, and sound libraries help build sound schools—the kinds of schools that provide us with a high level of "national intelligence."

PUBLIC SCHOOLS: STRENGTHENING DEMOCRACY AT THE LOCAL LEVEL

As Singer (2017) noted, public schools serve many purposes that are often forgotten. For example, our nation's schools frequently are the heart of the communities they serve. They offer extracurricular activities for youth, such as sporting events and academic clubs, often providing public use of swimming pools, tennis courts, and baseball fields—facilities for community activities. They invite community members to school events, such as concerts, plays, and seminars. They also support continuing education courses for adults, especially in immigrant communities. Such activities contribute to the health of our communities and thus the health of our democracy.

Singer also notes that public school systems recognize diverse community needs and, for years, have provided residents with a choice of schools. Today, the word "choice" seems to have been appropriated by those running private, voucher, or charter schools, but urban districts have offered magnet or theme schools for decades. Furthermore, public schools typically offer a wide variety of classes and curricula, providing students with choices in foreign language, or choices of vocational and technical curricula, as well as choices in the arts and humanities.

Public schools also regularly provide access to independent studies, advanced placement, and college credit courses. In addition, students can take advantage of a plethora of services that personalize their academic experience, such as enrollment in special or gifted education. In short, as *public* entities, public school districts and schools offer a great deal of the choice that young people and their parents need and want. Unregulated and unsupervised private schools, and many voucher or public charter schools, are not as likely to offer the same variety of choices.

Compared to private schooling, public education frequently has something else needed in American democracy—a diverse student body. John Dewey noted decades ago that schooling is life itself—it is not separate from life. Thus, students learn a lot more than reading, writing, and arithmetic in the public schools they attend; they learn how to interact with different kinds of people. They learn to share the world with humans from various racial, ethnic, and religious backgrounds, as well as those with different sexual identities. It is quite likely that the more diverse the environment our youth grow up in, the better adjusted they become as adults. Graduates from these environments are often less racist, sexist, and prejudiced than those who attend schools with homogenous student bodies, as is regularly found in charter, voucher, private, and religious schools (Peshkin, 1986).

Singer (2017) also pointed out that public schools are more fiscally responsible. Compared to private schools, public school expenditures are precisely that—public! Thus, the likelihood is greater that they will spend money more wisely than would charter or voucher schools. This is partly because their fiscal records are an open book, as should be the books of any organization receiving the public's money. In the rare instances where public school employees break the law and try to embezzle funds, they are much more likely to be caught because fiscal records are readily accessible.

It is important to realize that because public schools use taxpayer dollars, they belong to us, the people. Thus, if any citizen wants to exert their authority, they can usually do so. In a sense, public schools are run by our friends, neighbors, and co-workers. These "locals" live in our neighborhoods and sit on our school boards, parent-teacher associations and organizations (PTAs, PTOs), and advisory councils, all run by local folks. That is not necessarily true of charter, voucher, and private schools, which are more typically run by appointed boards of directors who may not be local. Whoever they are, they certainly are not beholden to local citizens or parents (Berliner, 2022). The administrators and boards of these schools are more likely to be a school's owners and investors. Parents and local citizens can find reaching them challenging, compared to their experiences with public schools.

Public schools accept donations, and sometimes teachers ask for help, but if parents cannot (or will not) send in such things as pencils or tissues, the school provides it, *gratis*. When a district does not (or cannot) provide what is needed, teachers will often make up the difference from their own pockets (Litvinov, 2022). On average, public school teachers spend over $500 each year on their classrooms. In private and charter schools, this rarely happens. Furthermore, special education and gifted child programs rarely exist in these schools. In our nation's public schools, such programs are common, and they are often first-rate. Additionally, public schools provide transportation (school buses, vouchers for public transportation, etc.), which private and charter schools rarely provide.

Another admirable characteristic of public schools is their reliability. Neighborhood public schools will almost always be there. This is not necessarily true of charter and voucher schools. When you send your child to those schools, you never know if they will be there tomorrow (Sandoval, 2015). They open and close regularly.

Yet another difference between public schools and private, voucher, and charter schools is that they do not have to accept your child (Simon, 2013). Public schools do. They are required by law to educate every child in their district, including homeless children and those who are disabled. Only under extreme circumstances do public schools expel a young person. Indeed, there are public school scandals about *who* is expelled and *why*. Investigations of these incidents frequently expose systemic bias and racism among teachers and school leaders. But that's the point. It's not that public schools do not sometimes do awful things; it is that *the actions of the public schools become public*! Charter and voucher schools can keep their prejudices hidden and intact.

Data collected worldwide suggest that the frequent advantage of charter, voucher, and independent private schools on standardized achievement tests, when compared to public schools, is because of *who* attends those schools. It is *not* because their curriculum or their instruction are superior. More likely, family wealth and social class status are the more powerful determinants of their test scores. Of note is that when the socioeconomic characteristics of public and nonpublic school attendees are statistically controlled, public school students academically outperform private, charter, and religious school students (Berliner & Biddle, 1995; Lubienski & Lubienski, 2014). Thus, public schools are not only far more likely to teach for democratic living effectively, but students also do better academically.

AUTHORITARIAN NATIONS AND EDUCATION

This essay opened with my ChatGPT query about how our public schools contribute to democracy. I also asked ChatGPT, "What is the role of education in an authoritarian nation?" The answer I received is just as predictable as was the answer about the role our public schools play in a democracy. Developing a consensus from millions of pages of scanned text, ChatGPT stated that the role of schools in authoritarian nations is the maintenance of power by a political administration. Schools in these societies function to control its citizens. In America's almost 100,000 public schools, we must always guard against the techniques of those authoritarian schools that ChatGPT has identified, schools where we can expect to see excessive control of behavior; limits on information that is shared; propaganda more frequent than fact in courses on history, civics, and government; and limits on the expression of dissent.

CONCLUSION

ChatGPT was quite clear about the positive relationship between U.S. public schools and our American democracy. But I pointed out that when public schools focus their curriculum on employability, it may not be as good for democracy as promoting learning for life and for active participation. Second, I made the argument that students learn democratic ideology and the critical thinking skills needed to be informed, active citizens if they are allowed a bit of freedom to self-initiate some curricula choices, and investigate deeply topics of interest to them. Third, I argued that democracy is difficult to teach and learn about in schools that do not run as democratic institutions. In too many of America's schools it is harder, if not impossible, for students to see democracy in action. Fourth, I noted that the relationship between students learning about our democracy and school accountability that relies heavily upon standardized testing is rarely discussed. When districts and administrators emphasize school and student accountability, students are less likely to be engaged in democratic thinking and acting. Typically, issues about education for democracy are not debated by, nor is it a priority of, those making educational policy. Furthermore, school disruptions due to the recent COVID-19 pandemic and new liability laws have negatively affected learning for democratic living by limiting access to extracurricular experiences, such as field trips and school visits from those who make our democracy work (government officials, firefighters, police officers, etc.).

Finally, I addressed the recent verbal and physical attacks on educators and librarians, and book banning, all of which are antidemocratic actions. Particularly worrisome is the expressed desire by some parents and politicians to ignore or punish youth when issues related to gender identity or political organizing by students arise. Of concern is that our students are too often observing nondemocratic adult models, and youth learn from adult models. This does not bode well for the future of our democracy. On a positive note, however, schools are intricately tied to their communities. Their contributions to communal democratic ways of life are inestimable.

Both democratic and nondemocratic forces are always at play in our schools. They always have been. But I fear that in today's political environment, we may be seeing too many nondemocratic ways of living together and schooling our children. We need more thought about this, because as the twig is bent, so grows the child.

Culling and Cream Skimming

Things We Do to Herds and With School Children in Charter and Private Schools*

To cull is to select things you intend to reject, often in reference to a group of animals. An outbreak of hoof-and-mouth disease can lead authorities to order a cull of farm pigs. An outbreak of low test scores or a meeting with undesirable parents can promote the culling of a charter or private school student.

Cream skimming is meant to remove something choice from an aggregate, such as pursuing the healthiest clients for an insurance company, or the healthiest patients for a hospital. Cream skimming in education is about selecting the best and the brightest, and/or the most docile-appearing students and families, for acceptance into a charter or private school.

My colleague, the eminent educator Diane Ravitch, was criticized for writing that charter schools, supported by public tax money, engage in culling and cream skimming students and their families. But she was right. Public charter schools and private schools that accept public monies through vouchers frequently admit only certain students, often those predicted most likely to succeed, and whose parents are "acceptable." And if these schools choose "wrong," they simply cull the herd. Between selective admissions through cream skimming, and culling, the data frequently used to describe a school's accomplishments makes charter and voucher schools look quite good, compared to public schools, who accept all who apply and who keep working with almost all of the students in their care. Thus, the apparent success of charter and private voucher schools is almost always an illusion. In fact, comparisons between nonselective public schools and schools that select their students cannot ever be sensibly made because the differences are just too great.

Let me illustrate what those differences look like first with data collected by my wife, Dr. Ursula Casanova. She wrote in the *Washington Post* about

---

*An earlier version of this essay appeared online at Diane Ravitch's blog on April 13, 2020: https://dianeravitch.net/2020/04/13/david-berliner-how-successful-charter-schools-cull-and -skim-students-they-dont-want/)

the Basis (charter) school in Scottsdale, Arizona, enrolling students in grades 5–12 (Casanova, 2012). Based on its test scores that year, it was named the top high school in Arizona. But the year it was so honored, Casanova found enrollments from 5th through 8th grade to be 152, 138, 110, and 94, respectively. Clearly, over time, schoolchildren began disappearing. Then, the high school enrollments, in grades 9–11, numbered 42, 30, and 23, respectively. Finally, the 12th-grade graduating class of this school had eight students! With no shame whatsoever, the Basis school was able to claim they graduated 100% of their seniors and that all were accepted to college! Culling cattle or kids is certainly a time-tested way to improve the quality of the stock remaining!

The Basis school of Tucson, part of the same chain of over 20 charter schools in Arizona (as of 2021), presented data that year that showed a similar pattern. In the year for which Casanova reported, the school started out with 127 students in the 5th grade. But they had only 100 students in 8th grade, 69 in the 9th grade, 45 in 10th grade, and 27 in 11th grade. At the end of 12th grade, only 24 seniors were still there for graduation. The graduating class was only 35% of the 9th-grade cohort, and they were less than 20% of that 5th-grade cohort. For this school, and for this chain of schools, culling the herd seemed to be a favored policy!

My recent examination of Basis school enrollments, using 2019 public data, revealed that they have done better at student retention. Still, the Basis charter in Ahwahtukee, Arizona, had an enrollment at 5th grade of 116 students, but in 12th grade only 48 students attended. Similarly, in the Basis school in Peoria, Arizona, enrollment in 5th grade was 196, which had dropped to 48 by 12th grade. Perhaps this is just natural attrition. But it seems more likely that these publicly supported charter schools are (a) failing the parents who chose to send their children to this school, who then pull their children out; or (b) culling students and families—something a genuine public school would never do. Neither of these alternatives suggests a legitimately successful school.

Another likely example of culling comes from Philadelphia's Boys Latin Charter, designed to be a high-prestige academic charter school for Black students. Boys Latin proudly boasted that 98% of its students were accepted into college. But Jersey Jazzman (2017) found that in the years 2011–2015 the school graduated about 60% of its 9th-grade class, culling approximately 40% of its student body, and thus allowing the school to make a claim that almost all of its students are college-bound. That claim may be true, but only because of odious school policies.

My former student Amy Potterton wrote about four highly rated charter schools in Arizona, two from the Basis schools chain, the same chain mentioned above, and two other schools from the Great Hearts Academy chain, which administered over 20 schools in the Phoenix area (Potterton, 2013). In the year of her study, Potterton found that the average rate for free and reduced lunch in Arizona schools was 35%. The average for free and reduced lunch in these four charter schools? 0%, 0%, 0%, 0%! Could there be cream skimming going on? Some kind of illegal selection bias? That same year the state average for English language learners in Arizona schools was 7.5%. The English language learners in these four schools? 0%, 0%, 0%, 0%! Any chance that cream skimming was going on? It sure looks like that to me!

More evidence of this possibility arises from an analysis of special education enrollments in the state. In Arizona, as in all states, students with special needs are identified. Individualized Education Programs, IEPs, are prepared for those students. An IEP alerts school personnel that a child has been assessed and found to be in need of some form of special education, to which federal law entitles them. A simple accommodation may suffice, e.g., more time for completing a test. But major and expensive accommodations may also be required by law, e.g., assistance with learning in all subjects or mobility assistance. Either of these accommodations might require a full-time aide. Thus, special education children can be expensive children to have at a school. And expensive children are not wanted by charter or voucher schools even though they receive public funding for their private, largely unregulated, businesses. My colleague Anthony Garcy studied this issue empirically. He found that as the severity of a students' disability increased, the probability that they were enrolled in a charter school, rather than a public school, decreased (Garcy, 2011). Such children simply were too expensive to teach! Potterton's (2013) data seal this case. Arizona students identified as in need of special education averaged 12% in the year of her study. But the percentage of special education students in the four "outstanding" schools that Potterton studied was between .06% and 3.5%!

Arizona's ACLU in 2017 noted that state law forbade charter schools from limiting the number of special education students they accept. But The Rising School in Tucson advertised blatantly that the school's special education and resources department "is currently full. . . . Thus, any student with an IEP will be put on our waiting list." Similarly, AmeriSchools Academy (in Phoenix, Tucson, and Yuma) blatantly noted that "Special Education placements are limited to a capacity of ten (10) students for each school site. Students in excess of this number are to be wait listed with provisional registration." These statements were made in complete defiance of state law, which forbids schools that accept public funding from discriminating against special education students. Apparently, no elected official in Arizona cared to prosecute the selective admission policies of these schools. And of course, the more selective a school's admission policy, the less likely it will need to cull.

Furthermore, by state law, charter schools in Arizona may not require students or their parents to complete pre-enrollment activities, such as essays, interviews, or school tours. Nor can charter schools use students' performance on interviews or essays to determine which students to accept. But the ACLU of Arizona found that at the Flagstaff Arts and Leadership

Academy students *must* write a one-page essay as part of their enrollment application. As part of the enrollment process at the Satori Charter School in Tucson, parents and students *must* meet with a school administrator. These are all excellent, *though completely illegal* ways to eliminate undesirable children and families from ever getting into these publicly supported schools! Culling can be greatly reduced, of course, if you can keep the people you don't want to serve from ever entering your schools!

Selective admissions and culling policies at a publicly supported religious schools are so well tolerated by state authorities in North Carolina that it is all done openly! For example, the Fayetteville Christian School in North Carolina was the recipient, in a recent school year, of $495,966 of public money. But despite its public funding, it is *not* open to the public (Fayetteville Christian School, n.d.)! Its admission policy is on the web and quite explicit. They say, up front, that it doesn't want Jews, Muslims, Hindus, and many others as students. At this school, they require that a student, and at least one parent, take Jesus Christ as their personal savior. Otherwise, a student will not be admitted to this school. Moreover, neither students nor their parents can engage in sexual promiscuity, illicit drug use, or homosexuality—or any other activity that scripture (in the school's view) defines as deviant or perverted. Any report of such activities by parents or the students is grounds for expulsion. So here, culling of the student body is based upon religion and lifestyle, including the lifestyle of a students' parents or guardians, in a school receiving then about a half million dollars per year of public funds!

Usually, state law directs charter schools *not* to require parental involvement as a condition of admission. And furthermore, charter schools must not pressure parents into donating money for the support of the school. As is true of all states, the Arizona Constitution guarantees students the right to a free public education. And charter schools call themselves public schools because they are, indeed, supported by public funds. But the ACLU of Arizona (2017) found that the same Great Hearts Academy charter schools reported on above asked each family to contribute $1,500 per student per year. Parents were also encouraged to donate anywhere from $200 to $2,000 to the school. The Montessori Day Public School chain noted that "All parents are expected to contribute 40 hours of volunteer time per family, per year." The Freedom Academy in Phoenix and Scottsdale required a nonrefundable $300 "Extracurricular Arts Fee," due at enrollment. My personal favorite lawbreaker is the San Tan Charter School in Gilbert, Arizona. They required parents to provide a credit card the school can keep on file to pay several fees, including a $250 technology rental fee for grades 9–12. Each school I mentioned, *in defiance of law*, found effective ways to openly cream skim and to cull families.

Many of the schools I have mentioned above have reputations as "excellent" public charter or "great" voucher-supported private schools. Their reputations are good because their standardized achievement test scores are high. Rather than excellence in curriculum and instruction, their reputation reflects their selective admissions and culling. In fact, many of these schools have much lower rates of certified teachers, and much higher teacher turn-over rate. Thus, it is more likely that these schools have a larger staff of inex-perienced teachers than would a regular public school. Research tells us that teachers get better at what they do every year over their first 10 years on the job (Kini & Poldosky, 2016). So if it wasn't for the culling and cream skim-ming of students and families, these schools might well have much lower standardized test scores than they ordinarily demonstrate. So it seems that culling and cream skimming really do pay off in terms of a school's aca-demic reputation, especially in states like Arizona that will not administer their own laws. In such circumstances, of course, democracy withers, and perhaps it even dies!

When Dr. Casanova (2012) reported on the clear evidence of culling in Arizona's charter schools, she asked an excellent question of our state's citi-zenry. She not only reported on the graduation rates of various charter and private schools, but also compared them to the reports from San Luis High School in San Luis, Arizona, on the Mexican border, which is part of the Yuma, Arizona, school system. Data from different state and local sources in-form us that in the years around the time she studied the charters, this public high school was serving almost 3,000 students a year, almost 100% of whom were Hispanic, half of whom were limited English proficient, and most of whom were classified as economically disadvantaged. But this *genuine* pub-lic high school managed to graduate over 80% of their freshman class, and almost 90% of its senior class! They also were able to do this with a teacher/pupil ratio well in excess of the U.S. average, and working with Arizona's per pupil school funding formula, which was, and still is, among the lowest in the nation. Why isn't San Luis High School, and others like it, considered among our great American high schools, compared to charter and voucher schools that brazenly and illegally cull and cream skim to look good on state achievement tests?

To see if Casanova's glowing report and thoughtful question about this school still hold, I checked the 2019–2020 data set for this school, obtained from the Arizona Department of Education (AZ School Report Cards, 2020). Enrollment at San Luis High from 9th to 12th grade was 686, 661, 678, and 698, respectively! A gain, not a loss of students. Moreover, 99.7% of the nearly 2700+ students were Hispanic. Yet their 4-year graduation rate is 93%, and their college attendance rate is 60%. Their enrollment in Advanced Placement (AP) courses was 652. No cream skimming, no culling, just good old American, doors-open-to-all public education, delivered by means of committed and well-trained teachers, counselors, and administrators.

We must not fail to note something else that is egregious about Amer-ica's charter and voucher schools, namely, that when these schools receive their state money, it's almost always at the expense of the states' education budget for public schools. The total amount of funding for schools in a state is rarely increased, almost never keeping pace as the numbers of schools in the state goes up. So schools that break the laws of the state to gain a good academic reputation through objectionable means are getting a significant part of the educational funding provided by the public for its *genuine* public schools. A genuine public school like San Luis High School—with certified teachers, transportation, counselors, nurses, food services, social workers, special education teachers, bilingual staffing, athletics, music, art, and drama—receives less than it might otherwise. And, of course, it will have higher per-pupil costs than a charter or voucher school that provides no such services or activities. Using a similar funding formula for both kinds of schools is, therefore, inherently unfair. But such is modern America, where unfair educational policies are promoted in many states, and embraced warmly by far too many inequalitarian politicians, who believe that anything "private" is good, and anything "government" is not.

Many of our genuine public schools deserve our nation's gratitude for the good job they are doing educating our youth, many of whom live under difficult conditions. Remember, so difficult are the circumstances of some children that most of our charters and voucher schools *won't even attempt to teach them*! These charter and private school "undesirables" are the very students our regular public schools accept and work with day in and day out. Such students are not dismissed because they are difficult to teach; instead, they are supported, counseled, and given second and third chances. I don't think it is too far a reach to think that public school teachers, like America's clergy, are in the business of saving souls! Teachers don't just teach to the gifted students, and our clergy do not just preach to the saved. Teachers and clergy try to help them all.

In opposition, so common to charter and voucher schools, is the Darwinian approach designed to systematically push the weakest or most difficult to teach students out of school. This should be abhorrent to the citizens and legislators of a democracy. But a kind of Darwinism really is the philosophy guiding some of our nation's highest-rated charter and voucher schools. For example, a respondent to a blog by my colleague Gene V Glass, where he too criticized the culling and cream skimming of charters, stated the following: "Basic schools do not engage in any form of thinning across any grade. Students do drop out because *they are not fit to thrive in the difficult curriculum. . . .*"

Let's think about what "not fit to thrive" in the environment of a common school might look like as a guiding philosophy for our nation's public schools. We could do away with special education, bilingual education, counseling and guidance, transportation, free and reduced-cost meals, school nurses, and so forth. The Darwinian approach to schooling is not merely undemocratic, it is vile! And so, I could not have been more pleased to see such evil confronted in an American court. In March 2021, a U.S. district court ruled that the Success Academy Charter chain—which advertises that it is open to all children—must pay $2.4 million to a small group of parents whose 4- and 5-year old special education children were forced out of their schools (Ravitch, 2021). If it were me, I wouldn't give another public dollar to any charter or voucher school that culls and skims the cream. They are all patently undemocratic institutions running on public money. But the issue is even bigger. Since there is so little oversight of charter and voucher schools—either in how they spend their public dollars or in how they educate our children—I really wouldn't support any of them at all unless they were regularly audited and inspected as all public institutions ought to be (Berliner, 2022).

Parents! Chill Out!

Learning Losses in the "Required" School Curriculum Are Easily Offset by Gains Made in the "Not Required" Curriculum

I began writing this essay during the worst of the COVID-19 pandemic and lockdown, when parents expressed concerns that their children had not, or would not, learn enough through their participation in the non-standard styles of schooling associated with the pandemic. Some worried, particularly, that their children would not test well if they missed too much of what we came to regard as "regular" schooling. The regular or standard school curriculum differs only slightly by state, but this curriculum is what state and local school boards approve, and what teachers try to deliver in each grade. The standards developed in each state are designed to prepare children for their state's annual achievement tests and to prepare students for the SATs and ACTs, taken near the end of high school by students planning to go to college. For many years now, in most countries, the "regular school curriculum" has been described in considerable detail for students at each grade level. In fact, 200 years ago, Napoleon Bonaparte expressed the hope that any French citizens could pull their watch from their pocket, at any time of day, and tell precisely what was being taught at any grade in every school in the country! Missing any of that state-approved/-required curriculum could, indeed, lead to some loss in test scores 200 years ago, and now.

But Napoleon's desire to have everyone learn the same thing at the same time, and contemporary parents worrying about their children not learning enough, triggered, in my mind, educational settings reminiscent of Chaplin's prescient movie *Modern Times*, where Charlie cannot keep up with the conveyer belt that brings him more, and still more, and even more, to do. With so many expressions of concern about children being slowed down, I was also reminded of my recent visit to an Amazon sorting and packing center, which looked a bit like Chaplin's factory. I began having visions of everything in industry and education being sped up, overwhelming workers, as well as teachers and students alike, in order to achieve the goals of factory managers, school superintendents, principals, and the politicians to whom they all answer. Workers, teachers, students, be damned: More, ever more, needs to be done, and it all needs to be done faster, ever faster!

The Common Core of learning, now a major part of almost every state's curriculum focus, has some of these unfortunate qualities. Standardization of what is to be learned, how much is to be learned, in what sequence, and at which grade level, was promoted by past state and federal administrations, and expanded during the first Trump term. It is actually the antithesis of what I hope our students might experience in our public schools. I am as sure as John Dewey that current educational practices—the desire for uniformity of curriculum and for common standardized assessments—will stifle spontaneity and creativity in both teaching and learning. In fact, it was Dewey who once expressed that the school curriculum ought to be anything a student wanted to learn. That may be too radical for most of us, but perhaps a part of the school curriculum could be devoted to anything a student wanted to learn or to some project of use or of interest to students and, potentially, their communities.

I would like parents and educators to stop worrying about learning the "required stuff" in the ordinary, test prep–oriented curricula now in place in most American districts and schools. Instead, I'd like them to just think about our youth simply learning "good stuff." A lot of educational problems disappear if we all stop worrying about learning everything that might be on the tests, and worry instead that each student learned a lot of good stuff. Period! Full stop!

Learning, growing intellectually, forming beliefs that are fact-based, gaining deep insights into particular subject matters, extending one's horizons, and mastering something complex are what are important. Surely, we can all agree that there is a plethora of "stuff'" worth learning out there—stuff that is of interest, utility, or beauty. I bet we might also agree that huge amounts of these worthwhile things to learn are not in the accepted/normal/required/test prep–focused contemporary school curriculum. If we can agree that (1) there is a lot of good stuff to learn, and (2) lots of that good stuff never makes it into the ordinary school curriculum, then maybe we shouldn't worry about whether our students are learning the required curricula, *as long as they are learning other desirable and worthwhile things.*

With this thought in mind, you can see why I don't get as distressed as so many others do because COVID-19, or some other factor, caused some kids to miss the "proper" time in their development to learn this or that. I am not against learning what gerunds are, the role of apostrophes, long division and simple algebra, or the date that the Constitution was signed. These may all be worthy goals in youths' passage through our public schools to competent adulthood. But what if a substantial part of the thinking and learning they were engaged in at school was based, instead, on a project the student chose or was assigned and willingly accepted? What if a student had a topic to study and became highly knowledgeable about that area? And what if students must eventually report on their project or topic of study? If these kinds of activities were a central feature of schooling, what would be lost? What would be gained?

We now know that even 1st-graders are capable of learning sophisticated information about, say, dinosaurs. In fact, many of them do this spontaneously and are quite capable of knowing more about dinosaurs and the lives they led than the vast majority of adults (Chi & Koeske, 1983). There are lots of young chess experts, mathematicians, musicians, writers, scientists, and Civil War enthusiasts, among others. Each of them makes the case, over and over again, that deep and intense study of a topic is possible, even for young learners if they are interested in that topic. In fact, the evidence is overwhelming that sophisticated domain knowledge—the knowledge of experts—can be learned by schoolchildren who might choose or be assigned the study of rainfall, global warming, dog breeding, volcanoes, the life of a mosquito, or a thousand other topics. What if our children began to learn these other good things, as well as whatever online or regular instruction a teacher or school provides during a pandemic? What if this form of learning were provided in our schools during more normal times? Would America's children lose anything? Or might our students actually gain from such individualized learning experiences?

The beauty of the kinds of inquiries I am proposing is that there would be little downtime for students' education during a pandemic, or during other times schools are not in regular session—particularly during holidays. Many, perhaps most, students who are engrossed in a project or the study of a topic would learn about something of interest to them and possibly of interest to their community, but it wouldn't necessarily be in their states' required curriculum for their age group or grade. I became interested in this kind of learning as I drove my son, a high school freshman at the time, to 10 different sites around San Francisco Bay that gave access to Bay water. He needed water samples for a project he was doing. After he and two colleagues tested the water they had obtained, they issued two warnings to classmates: (1) It is not wise to swim in the Bay, and (2) Do not ever eat fish or seafood from the Bay! Their teacher and the boys were filled with pride when their research was published in a local newspaper. Project learning has great motivational properties if projects and students are matched appropriately, and these projects can serve useful purposes for the community.

It should be noted that in a pandemic, or in other times when schools are closed or limited in their instruction, the projects and reports I am talking about may well provide better evidence for judging student competence than would any state achievement test. That is because when students have not all been exposed to the "regular" curriculum—the curriculum from which our achievement tests are derived—the test is prima facie invalid. Standardized tests in these unusual times may not claim "content validity." That is, if students have not all been exposed to the content represented in the test, the test scores are uninterpretable. Under these conditions, test results are largely invalid for many of the purposes for which they were created. Although student assessments of the "required" curriculum are not likely to be valid, perhaps students can be assessed on their learning of some of the "not required" curriculum. These are the projects and reports they can do in lieu of studying for the tests that assess the required curriculum but are no longer the actual curriculum.

Under all circumstances, we want our students to learn a lot of "good stuff." Especially if they are limited in their access to the "required stuff." Learning something in depth, and sharing it with others, may be an excellent replacement for the learning loss in the "required stuff" that occurs any time there are school closures because of pandemics, hurricanes, tornadoes, school strikes, summer break, Christmas, acts of violence, and the like. But I want to emphasize that what I suggest next is likely good for normal times, not just for the times when schools are shut down.

A closer look at project-based learning. Imagine if one, or a few students, had some months to turn in a project on whether the air or water in their community is breathable or drinkable; the climate is changing in their community; their schools are adequately funded; their food is safe to eat; or a robot could be built to help the cafeteria staff at their school. Or perhaps the students investigated the causes of homelessness or asthma or the need for public transportation in their community. There exists an almost endless supply of challenging projects, local and otherwise, worthy of study. Many will be appropriate for a particular age group, and some will require sustained effort over a moderately long time period to master the material at an age-appropriate level. A project not only teaches an individual but, if done with another student, can also substantially remove the feelings of loneliness that many of our students feel during school closures. Moreover, two things are frequently noticed when students present their research projects or topical research to peers, teachers, and parents. First, students show evidence that they have learned how to organize and reorganize their ideas to prepare presentations from which others could learn—if not the first time they do it, soon thereafter. Second, their presentations almost always demonstrate that deep learning in the domain of study has taken place. The remarkable educator Debbie Meier (1995) describes successful schools where this approach has happened on a regular basis. The schools she describes didn't wait for a crisis to incorporate the idea that children can direct their own learning, with the help of some adult scaffolding. Her experience, and the testimony of others who studied the schools she directed, convincingly established that students can and do dig deeply and happily into subject matter that they want to learn and share with others! Dear reader, did you ever know stuff that others didn't? What power that gives! Proposed here are ways in which every child gets a chance to be the authority, the all-knowing one, the expert, about something whether it be tuna or Tunisia, the Great War or the Great Migration, arterial roads, or coronary arteries!

Topics to study. The topics investigated by a particular student might be of interest to them or even assigned. If students cannot find a project to work on, they can work with their teachers to find a topic: Birds, automobiles, penguins, glaciers, honeybees, artificial intelligence, the Civil Rights Movement, internment camps during World War II, comets, Colorado River water rights, and so forth. The student's job is to become expert in that topic and present a talk on that topic to their classmates and others when they are ready to convey what is exciting and important to know about that topic. A very different version of how this approach might work schoolwide and across grades is described by the very creative philosopher of education Kieran Egan (2011). New York City has special schools and programs designed for project-based learning (NYC Outward Bound Schools, n.d.), as do America's many 4H clubs (Ponzio & Fisher, 1997). In fact, the 4H clubs have successfully used project-based science learning for decades. I am suggesting such ideas be made more mainstream, and that they be a part of the ordinary public school curriculum.

If learning from projects and topical studies as I have described were made more salient in the educational experiences of our youth, while the ordinary/standard curriculum were taught whenever and however it could be taught, what might happen? We actually have some data related to this kind of arrangement. It comes from a classic, long-term, highly creative study conducted many years ago (Aiken, 1942; see also *The High School Journal*, 1942). As the push to standardize the American curriculum gained traction, history has forgotten this study. But it is still quite instructive.

In that study, students in 30 unique high schools, "progressive" schools, were studied. These 30 schools had agreed to let their students take a nonstandard curriculum. The students studied some of what the school wanted them to, as current online instruction is meant to do. But these students also received high school credits for choosing to study, think, write about, and build almost anything they wanted. The high school gave them credits for doing some highly unusual, self-determined projects and papers, few of which would have been approved had these students been subject to the standard high school curriculum of their time.

The hundreds of students attending these progressive schools, taking a very *nonstandard* high school curriculum, went on to about 300 colleges and universities, all of which had agreed to monitor and document their progress and achievements. The universities were also to monitor these students' deficits as well, since they had not been "properly prepared" for their college experience. They clearly had not studied the regular, standard, state-sanctioned curriculum, so it appeared that it would be difficult for them to compete in college.

From the major reports of this study, we learn that at whatever college they attended, each of the progressive school graduates was matched with a traditional school graduate who shared many similar background characteristics. Subsequent analyses showed that the graduates of "progressive" schools: showed more leadership; joined and led more clubs; were rated as thinking more clearly; demonstrated a better understanding of democracy; had greater interest in good books, music, and art; and got slightly better grades in their colleges than those from traditional schools. They won more academic honors, as well (e.g., Phi Beta Kappa and honor roll designations). A special sub-study of the graduates of the six *most* progressive schools, what traditionalists thought of as the "wildest" of the schools, revealed that in college those students were superior to their peers from the other progressive schools! Thus, they scored well above the traditionally educated students on all the indices used for comparison. These "inadequately educated" students, deprived of the regular/standard/normal state-sanctioned curriculum, actually achieved the highest college grades, and were also rated the highest in intellectual drive, highest in thinking ability, and highest in extracurricular activity participation.

All I have written on this topic above now comes down to this: The scholars reporting on the 8-year study said that the belief that *students must have a prescribed school curriculum is not tenable*. They said, and I believe, that studying almost anything in depth and breadth, with some (but not necessarily a lot of) teacher support, and reporting it out, prepares a child for the highest levels of scholarship at the next levels of their learning. There were no apparent negative effects from studying "this," instead of "that," if it was studied well. Learning seriously, deeply, and sharing that knowledge through papers and presentations (perhaps with PowerPoint and YouTube, maybe via film, television, music, or art) to one's peers, parents, and the school faculty apparently has no long-term ill effects, when compared to learning the "required" curriculum.

So to all the worried parents, teachers, and school administrators concerned that our youth will not learn at the proper time in their development about gerunds and the role of apostrophes, or long division and simple algebra, or the date the Constitution was signed, relax! Chill out! Let us instead make sure our children are learning good stuff through projects and topics that capture their fancy during the time they do have. That should more than suffice for what they might miss of the traditional curriculum during times of pandemics, or when any other crisis limits their learning of the traditional/required curriculum.

My Incredibly Short Career as a Brain Surgeon and Some Thoughts About Teaching

When I was an undergraduate psychology major at UCLA, I studied physiological psychology, particularly neuroanatomy. During my master's program at California State College, Los Angeles I landed a job as a research assistant at the UCLA brain research center. There, I did some fascinating studies of brain functioning. Well, more accurately, my job was to get some rats drunk and then test them. I gave the rats a little alcohol, then I had a little alcohol, then they got a bit more, and then I . . . well, I am sure you get the picture. I continue to read my physiological psychology textbooks, and in addition have found the works of Oliver Sachs and A. S. Luria to be wonderful reading. In fact, it was Sachs's engaging *The Man Who Mistook His Wife for a Hat* that inspired me to write essays such as this.

I note also that I frequently buy and avidly read whatever popular science magazines come out featuring stories about the brain. I am up on CAT scans and fMRIs and the latest techniques for stroke victims, and much, much more. Just as important as all the technical knowledge I possess is the fact that I also have a flair for carving, a skill attested to by anyone who has had Thanksgiving dinner with my family.

Naturally, with such interest, such knowledge, and such skills, I have always thought that I would make a great brain surgeon. My secret fantasy was to become the greatest brain cartographer of modern times, locator of Berliner's spot, or the Berliner bundle. I secretly dreamed I could eventually locate and describe how memory works—a goal of every psychologist.

Then, out of the blue, the most wonderful opportunity arose. I discovered that there was a chance that I could get to be a brain surgeon after all. I might actually be able to practice my real vocational love. This wonderful and exciting change in my life, one that I had dreamed about for so long, was suddenly within my grasp because that day, my newspaper ran a feature story on the scarcity of surgeons at the hospitals serving the most impoverished members of our society. One of our largest state-supported big-city hospitals complained that it was short of neurosurgeons all week. Furthermore, on weekends, in the emergency rooms, they *never* had a specialist on whom to call.

My local newspaper, for many years, took a conservative, free-market approach to the economy. So, over the years, it has often been in favor of deregulating just about everything, particularly teaching. On the day I was reading about the shortage in the emergency room my newspaper ran an editorial on socialism in the United States using the "inefficient public school system" as their model. They cited someone who believed that "government schools" were founded on Marxist-Leninist principles. America's schools, the paper continued, were failures when measured against the rest of the world or against the results of private schooling. The newspaper's solution was more free enterprise, including vouchers for children, having schools compete with one another, and the closing of the useless schools of education. They, and one of our many Arizona governors who ended up in prison, eventually argued that anyone with a bachelor's degree could teach because teaching wasn't all that complicated.

Our newspaper was then owned by the Pulliam family. That is the family that gave America the well-known intellectual vice-president Dan Quayle. It was he who said, among other things, that his goal was to have as few government regulations as possible. Quayle's views, the news from the hospital, and the editorial seemed to provide the perfect set of conditions for propelling me into the career I always wanted. I actually shivered with hope and excitement.

It was time for people with my kinds of skills to step in and serve where clear social needs had been identified. What we needed was a resurgence of volunteerism to renew the spirit of America. And so I went to the hospital that had reported the shortages and volunteered to take the neurosurgery rounds on weekends.

I told them I hold a doctor's degree (well, actually, I really do have three doctorates, but I thought they would rebel if I asked them to call me Dr. Dr. Dr.). I informed them that I have a high level of knowledge about brain functioning and understood perfectly the technologies that existed to examine brains, and, with false modesty, I also told them that I really could carve quite well. While the hospital administrator was weighing my offer, I thought: "By golly, this is it, my big chance. I may be able to change careers overnight and make my dear mother posthumously ecstatic, by becoming a 'real' doctor."

I sat there waiting, thinking that if computer programmers can become high school teachers of mathematics overnight; if oil company geologists can become earth science teachers overnight; if mothers of two with bachelor's degrees in either home or international economics choose to enter the classroom when their youngest goes off to school and can get a job immediately, without any training beyond their life skills; and if military personnel of all kinds can get jobs in schools, and even jobs to run schools, immediately after they serve our nation, then I, with my skills and interest in neuroanatomy, should prove to be a great catch for the field of medicine. I knew I had what it takes and now here I was getting ready to demonstrate my talents. It was so exciting!

Alas. My hopes were quickly dashed. The administrator of the hospital informed me that they had no openings at that moment, but that one of their other physicians, a psychiatrist, would like to see me. I left quickly. I could tell he did not believe that I had enough knowledge and skill for the job, and I think that I sensed correctly that I could never convince him otherwise. I was crushed.

*   *   *

I don't know why, but for some strange reason people think that medicine is hard and teaching is easy. But let's look a little closer at that. A physician usually works with one patient at a time, while a teacher serves 25, 30, or more simultaneously in places like Los Angeles and other large cities. Many of these students don't speak English well. Typically, anywhere from 5–15% will show emotional and/or cognitive disabilities. Most are poor, and many reside in single-parent families. There is also another important difference in the motives of patients and students. Most patients seek out their physicians, choosing to be in their office. On the other hand, many students seek to get out of class, preferring the streets to classrooms that cannot engage them, and in which they often are made to feel inadequate.

I always wonder how physicians would fare if 30 or so kids with the kinds of sociological characteristics I just described showed up for medical treatment all at once, and then left 50 minutes later, healed or not! And suppose that chaotic scene were immediately followed by 30 or more different kids, but with similar sociological backgrounds, also in need of personal attention. And they too stayed about 50 minutes, and then they also had to leave. Imagine waves of these patients hitting a physician's office five or six times a day!

In addition, teachers are usually away from other adults for long segments of the day, with no one helping them, which makes possession of a strong bladder one of the least recognized attributes of an effective teacher. Physicians, on the other hand, often have a nurse and secretary to do some of the work necessary to allow them to concentrate on the central elements of their one-on-one practice. And they actually have time to relieve their bladders between patients, which helps improve their decision-making skills!

That so many teachers and schools do so well under the circumstances I have just described shows how undervalued the craft of teaching is, and how little respect there is for pedagogical knowledge. In fact, much of the knowledge needed for teaching and for successful medical treatment is clinical knowledge, or tacit knowledge, not easily described, and hard to teach to someone else. That's why physicians have grand rounds and a lengthy apprenticeship. Their prolonged apprenticeship is what gets them started learning what it means to be a *practicing* physician—rather than just a competent student of biology, chemistry, and pharmacology. Every clinician (psychologists, physicians, social workers, and teachers alike) knows that book learning can only teach a little slice of what it means to be a success in practice. The recognition of this fact is the quite sensible reason behind the requirement that teachers need to take teaching methods courses that instruct them in how to teach mathematics, how to teach phonics and comprehension skills, how science is learned, and so forth. Coursework in mathematics, English literature, and science have no more to say about the *teaching* of mathematics, literature, and physics than books on organic chemistry prepare a physician for their medical practice. Lengthy residencies are needed in medicine to learn to be a physician, and extensive student teaching is needed to become a competent teacher. Fields of complexity, with a strong element of art infusing their practice, and with much of their knowledge base being tacit, require prolonged time to learn even the minimum, and much longer to to achieve competence on a regular basis.

They won't let me be a brain surgeon because I have none of the tacit knowledge needed to go along with my book knowledge, interest, desire to serve the public, and, of course, my superb carving skills. I can accept that. But why the hell would anyone think it's different in education?

Please—let's keep untrained but good-hearted people out of classrooms until and unless they get some training in how to do that complex job well. Classroom teaching is hard work, noble work, and in some way, the life and death of our nation in a global economy depends on having competent people doing such work. The physician is literally, rather than figuratively, dealing with life and death. This gets them higher status, respect, and remuneration than our teachers get, but it is no more complex work, no more arduous, no more important to our nation, and certainly no more noble!

Let's be clear: Those who come into teaching from other fields have much to contribute. But not if we count their other experience as equivalent to studying about teaching methods, and not if their other experiences excuse them from an apprenticeship such as student teaching, which most regularly certified teachers have experienced. Regularly certified teachers usually take 12–16 weeks of supervised student teaching. Those coming into teaching from nontraditional routes, say those who enter teaching through the program called Teach for America (TFA), experience much less practice. The bright, young, highly motivated recent college graduates who join TFA ordinarily have 5 weeks of teaching experience with students who are *not* likely to be similar to those they actually end up teaching. Listen to Matt Brown, one of those bright, committed TFA recruits:

[W]hen I walked in that door to my trailer, I didn't have a freakin' clue. I had been a 1st grade teacher for five weeks [the training period] and . . . I had never taught more than two hours in a day. I didn't know how to set up a classroom, manage racial tensions, work with co-workers who weren't thrilled I was there, deal with parents, unit plan . . . really ANYTHING. I was eaten alive right from the start, and never really found my footing.

. . . The stresses of the constant failure of my work began to change me in ways I'm not so proud to admit. I started to find myself snapping at my students, punishing them to prove a point, or yelling more and more (in real life, I never yell . . . and seldom actually get angry). I used to get extremely stressed during certain parts of the day (say, when a troublemaking student would be in my room for an hour), but I gradually began to feel that way during the whole day . . . and then on my ride to school, and then even when I woke up on a weekday. Some days, I got to school two hours early, only to sit in the parking lot with the music on full blast, and my sunglasses on . . . so nobody would know I was crying. Other days, I threw up before going to school. Often, a particularly bad event at school could keep me upset for two days straight.

My former student and colleague Dr. Barbara Veltri provides much more documentation from other first-year underprepared teachers, all backing up Matt's story about the failure of so many TFA recruits in their initial year. That's why Veltri titled her oft-cited book *Learning on Other People's Kids* (2010). These are the poor, of course, those considered throwaway kids by the educational system: the kind of kids one learns to teach with. These are the ones on whom lots of mistakes are made, before moving out of the profession or on to schools with easier-to-teach children. By the way, it's really no different in medicine. Had I gotten my job as a brain surgeon I am sure I would have been working on the poorest people, where my "mistakes" would not have mattered as much! Our society does identify "lesser" humans, mostly the poor, and, therefore, frequently racially minoritized people, where inexperienced physicians and teachers are allowed to develop their skills. Higher rates of mistakes are permitted to be made with poor people, so that lower rates of mistakes will occur when dealing with "people of more substance!"

Perhaps the recognition of their incompetence, and their impotence in dealing with the overwhelming problems of poverty, are what drive many, like Matt, to leave the profession before their 2-year commitment is up. It is certainly likely that Matt didn't know, and his coaches didn't either because they lacked experience and were not scholars in education, that teachers have been found to make about .7 decisions *per minute* during interactive teaching (Borko & Shavelson, 1990). Another researcher estimated that teachers' decisions numbered about 1,500 per day (Jackson, 1990)! Decision fatigue is among the many reasons teachers are tired after what some critics call a short work day, forgetting or ignoring the enormous amount of time needed for preparation, for grading papers and homework, and for filling out bureaucratic forms and attending school meetings.

In fact, it takes about 10 years for teachers to reach their full ability to produce the most learning from their students (Kini & Podolsky, 2016). But about the time the TFA dilettante teachers start to get competent in their job, around their fourth year, 64% of the TFA recruits have left the profession, a much higher rate than among regularly certified teachers.

To be fair, however, the 36% of TFA recruits who stay longer in the field then they originally committed to, are most welcome additions to the profession. But as they gained in competency, they may have hurt a lot of poor children during their apprenticeship by fire!

Let's face it: People who want to practice medicine or education without sufficient training are ignorant, arrogant, or both. And those who would let them do so will only allow them to work with throwaway humans—the flotsam and jetsam found in many urban hospital emergency rooms, and the powerless poor in the impoverished schools of rural America, or in the the same urban neighborhoods as many of our "teaching" hospitals.

In education, we might think of legislators and accrediting bodies that allow untrained personnel to enter classrooms as traitors. Yes, a harsh pronouncement, I know, but the term fits. Persons who betray their country are correctly called traitors. The legislators, accrediting bodies, and chambers of commerce that endorse putting untrained or minimally trained teachers before poor children are hurting America, betraying the principles that Thomas Jefferson explicated 200 years ago. Jefferson, a slaveholder and not nearly as democratic as we might have wanted one of our founding fathers to be, did help to persuade his fellow founders of the nation that the poor have talent in equal degree as the rich. Thus, the poor deserved the same education as the rich, to cultivate those talents, so they can be used in service of the nation. He believed that the best way to preserve an ever-fragile democracy was a system of free public schooling. Those who would allow unqualified teachers to enter the classrooms of the poor are traitors to Jeffersonian principles.

Advocates of an "open market" in teacher certification are deliberately hurting America, and that, to me, is a traitorous act, especially since the research shows that teaching credentials do matter, and do actually lead to higher student achievement (Clotfelder et al., 2010). On top of that, most advocates for a free market in credentialing would never allow their own children to be taught by an untrained novice, or an inadequately trained teacher, nor would they allow their children to attend schools that rely heavily on such teachers. The hypocrisy and traitorous actions of legislators, business leaders, and policy analysts who advocate allowing anyone to teach in a school that would have them as teachers ensures that social class/social membership will remain as it is—difficult to modify. Moreover, the children most likely to be assigned teachers who have little or no training are children of color. So, on top of all my other charges, we might want to raise the issue of racism with the advocates of little or no credentialing for teachers. Traitors? Preservationists of the class structure? Racists? Wow! This is tough language for describing some of America's most noted politicians, businesspeople, and columnists. But until they put their own children in classes whose teachers are inadequately trained, I think it is fair to charge them with deliberately harming our nation. I'll apologize to these anti-teacher-credentialing groups when they let me operate on their family either as a teacher to their children or as a surgeon on their brain!

Providing Students an Opportunity to Acquire Expertise, and Teachers an Opportunity to Teach in Areas in Which They Possess Expertise

Most of us are familiar with the concept of opportunity to learn. Without opportunities to learn that which a society deems important, our youth will be unable to achieve the outcomes that are desired by our various state systems of education.

Providing the opportunity to learn the desired/approved/official school curriculum is a fundamental obligation of public education in contemporary America. States provide funding for the buildings, teachers, and texts so that the state-approved curriculum can be delivered to its students. But I have two thoughts about how limited that view might be. First, it may be quite desirable that students acquire expertise in areas of knowledge *beyond* what is offered up as the state-sanctioned/official curriculum. And, in addition, I also believe that teachers should have opportunities to teach that which they know deeply, find fascinating, and want to share with their students, even when it is not a part of the "official" state-sanctioned curriculum!

As important as it is to provide every student with an opportunity to learn curricula chosen for them by their state, I argue also that it is equally important to provide teachers with the opportunity to teach what they most want to teach—the knowledge, ideas, and insights they might care to share with their students. For a few hours here and there, every school year, teachers should be given the right, and be encouraged *if they so desire*, to choose curriculum they want to share with their students. Some part of the annual time allocated for instruction should be theirs, as long as what they propose to teach is broadly educational. These teaching opportunities should be fostered even if they are incompatible with the officially approved curriculum, and even if it interferes slightly with a class's preparation for a district's or a state's high-stakes tests.

In my experience, and perhaps in yours as well, there have been few learning activities as exciting as listening to an expert communicate about their area of expertise. Besides the vast knowledge experts have about some topic, curriculum area, or skill, they often have an enthusiasm that is communicated along with their descriptions of objects, processes, and events of interest. Furthermore, what experts communicate along with the "facts" of a situation, are the habits of mind—the ways of approaching problems, of thinking about issues, of accomplishing this or that—the characteristics that constitute the source of the experts' special knowledge and skill. This is true whether we are listening to an expert pianist, plumber, or parasitologist talk about their work.

Two personal experiences come to mind: The first occurred years ago, when I wandered into a western clothing store in Reno, Nevada, to accompany a friend who wanted to buy a western hat. There, an old cowboy gave us a lecture about and demonstration of hat-wearing styles like the "going-into-town on Saturday night" style. He also demonstrated how a reformed hat could be styled for rainy weather or shaped for bright sunshine. We learned that hats made of different materials, and the shapes they are formed into, are used for different kinds of activities engaged in by cowboys: posthole digging, riding, branding, racing, and roping. Each activity was associated with a preferred hat style. It really was quite memorable!

A second event occurred when I visited the home of an old friend. He had retired and taken up "shooting." I had no idea what that meant, and so we went to his workshop where he showed me how he packs powder into his own bullets, why his gun has a new sight, and why he changed from his older one. He also explained why he changed the stock on his gun and why he had to order a new barrel. He showed me his targets from every session he had spent at a shooting range over the previous few months. Every shot he took over those months was meticulously recorded in logs where the bullet size, weight, powder combinations, distance fired, and results were archived. My friend had become an expert! He not only taught me about this hobby or sport, but he also made me appreciate the intricacy, complexity, and challenges associated with what he did. I was thrilled to be taught by someone with deep knowledge and passion about their subject.

I think that deep knowledge and passion are the secret sauce behind engaging instruction for America's students! And it is precisely these characteristics that are often missing from classrooms faced with standardized achievement tests, which constrict both what is taught and what is learned.

I believe doctoral programs are most successful when more learning takes place in seminars and laboratories, rather than from lectures, textbooks, and testing regimes. History also informs us that many Nobel laureates were trained by other Nobel laureates, and that many great artists studied under other great artists. It is not just good networking that helps the younger individual to obtain recognition later in their career. It is also the fact that they studied with experts, and thus learned to think about, argue, and solve problems in a particular way within the domain in which they would later become famous. Listening to someone synthesize disparate bits of information to form something new, experiencing the habits of mind, the ways of thinking, the forms of argument, and the selectivity needed to decide what is important and what is not, are all the bits and pieces acquired from an acquaintance with experts.

Experts almost always have a richer and deeper understanding of that which brought them their notoriety than do others. In fact, research has shown that even young children who possess high levels of skills in music or chess, or youngsters who become experts about dinosaurs, the American Civil War, or insects, possess knowledge and have problem-solving skills far in excess of most adults who have only a passing acquaintance with these topics (Chi & Koeske, 1983).

For this and other reasons, the late philosopher of education Kieran Egan (2011) proposed to develop schools in which every child, from 1st grade on, has the chance to become an expert. Egan wanted every child afforded the opportunity to learn at least one domain deeply and have a chance to present their findings and ideas about their topic to the others in their class or school. Egan's proposal is almost totally ignored. But it really should be examined more seriously by school leaders.

What we now know about the acquisition of expertise suggests that after staying with a sport, an instrument, or a topic, because of external pressures—possibly from a coach, a parent, or a teacher—many novices enter a stage characterized by much more self-regulation (Glaser, 1996). At that time they practice an instrument or physical skill, read about some topic, or go on field trips to collect on their own, all without the external pressure that may have initially been needed to motivate them. The external motivation to practice or study eventually comes under intrinsic control. This is what some psychologists have described as "crossing the Rubicon." It is when motivation to learn comes under much greater volitional control (Corno, 1993). Crossing the Rubicon leads a learner into greater self-regulation of behavior. Volition, as opposed to external motivation, is a prominent factor in becoming an expert musician, athlete, scientist, mathematician, cake decorator, fashion designer, geographer, astronomer, farmer, magician, pilot, and other professions.

Egan had a plan to help students acquire expertise and thus to experience the joy of becoming expert at something. Knowing something better and more deeply than anyone else could well be a unique and wonderful learning experience for most students, and an ego builder for them, as well.

Egan believed that every student should have a subject assigned to them in the very early grades and stay with it for many years. These students should have sufficient time allotted to them to present their ever-growing knowledge of the domain they study to their classmates and the broader school community—parents and neighbors. This could be done at least once per year, perhaps starting with a 4- to 5-minute presentation in the early grades. In the later grades, presentations of a student's area of expertise could be 20 minutes or so. Many of the topics the students report on might well elicit interest from the broader adult community. It is an exciting plan for supplementing the required and often stultifying school curriculum.

If I were an influential educator, I would insist that the educational mission statement of every state say something like "It is the right of every child to experience the joy and power of possessing knowledge beyond that of almost all their contemporaries. And in addition, each child should be given the opportunity to share their knowledge with others."

In fact, were I to live out my fantasies as an influential educator, I would add: "It is the right of every teacher to provide instruction on anything they wanted, as long as it was a broadly educational subject that they loved, and in which they had expertise." Students have the right to experience passionate teaching and expertise by a teacher deeply committed to some domain of our human experience.

American educational policy does not now foster nor allow teachers the opportunity to teach what they know and love. In a study by Westerlund et al. (2002), a biology teacher in North Carolina says:

> Each one of us are specialists, each one of us has particular fields of study that we like, and [would] really like to impart more information to the kids. I love plants. I love teaching plants. I love teaching ecology. But currently I just skim over both of them because there are no plant questions on the end-of-course test. . . . You take what you like and you just PSHHT right by it, simply because you have to cover the goals and objectives of the state. And I don't like that. . . .

Isn't something wrong here? Is the state's curriculum that much better as preparation for life than the subject matter that Mr. Adams would teach? He said that if he did not have the high-stakes state test and the test preparation curriculum to contend with,

> I would just cover things that I enjoy more and feel like it would make me better in the classroom because the more you enjoy a particular aspect about a job you do, the better you are.

In this same study Ms. Henderson avers that she knows a lot about Venus flytraps, and the topic always fascinated her. But she cannot teach that anymore because it is not on the exams. The same study also quotes Ms. Langworthy, who had acquired expertise in fetal pig dissection, a subject that fascinated her students. But she, too, cannot teach that subject matter as part of her biology course. Nothing about that subject is on the state's test.

It is this loss of student exposure to expert knowledge that I mourn. It is a shameful waste of talent. Moreover, I don't think any of us is smart enough to know exactly what, in the official school curriculum, will make a difference in one's life after school—life in the real world. We all know that it is *not* just the scores obtained on standardized achievement tests that predict success after formal schooling is over (Deke & Haimson, 2006).

I ask myself if, instead of just learning primarily the required state and district curriculum, I might have been better off being exposed for a little bit of the school year to a teacher whose passion was sharing what they knew about collecting thimbles, medieval armaments, teacups, or butterflies. Would I be better off if some small percentage of my teacher's time was spent teaching me about the pigeons he kept on his roof, or the trip she took to Antarctica, or the cement boat he built, or listening to the teacher who stays up many nights to gaze through her high-powered telescope, looking for comets?

I think so. I think teachers should be given the opportunity to teach what they know deeply and love to teach, whether it is part of the "official" curriculum or not. I want to be sure that a literature teacher who loves *Moby-Dick* and understands the context for this great 19th-century American novel can teach their class what they know and what they find of interest in *Moby-Dick*, such as what the white whale may represent. If that teacher finds that *Moby Dick* is not on the list of approved readings and must teach, instead, *The Red Badge of Courage*, have their students lost something?

Of course, *The Red Badge of Courage* is more than "merely" worthwhile. It too is a great book. But has the class been cheated of the deep knowledge and passions of a teacher who would have been much happier to teach *Moby-Dick*? I think so! Whether a teacher's area of special expertise is a curriculum for English literature in the United States that is not all state-sanctioned, instruction in the life cycle of hummingbirds, or instruction about the Black jazz musicians who founded a baseball league in France after World War I really does not matter. If allowed, and urged to "strut their stuff," teachers are quite likely to provide their students with memorable educational experiences in topics about which those teachers possess deep knowledge.

Whether our students learn something useful or not, or are helped to pass achievement tests or not, should not be the only criteria for recommending curricula for classroom instruction. The opportunity to experience a growth of expertise in their own education and to experience instruction from an expert teacher are experiences likely to have independent positive effects on learners. For those who seem to forget, I remind you again: Neither a person, nor a nation's *tested* competencies in literacy, mathematics, and scientific knowledge, does a great job in predicting the future performance of either individuals or nations.

Perhaps then, allowing students the chance to develop expertise in whatever areas they are interested in or assigned, and having teachers teach something about the areas in which they possess expertise, is as good for assuring a successful future as is our push to have all our kids master the official/required/state school curriculum. Let's give students the gift of feeling extremely competent—of knowing more about some topic, year by year, than almost anyone else in their community! And let's give teachers a gift as well. Let's give them some opportunities to teach what they know deeply and might love to share. Perhaps if we did these things, we might have many more students and teachers feeling more efficacious, and a lot more satisfied with their experience in our public schools.

A Little Sociology and a Little Preaching About the New Kid on the Block

Compared to our European cousins, we in the United States change our residences frequently. On average, moving companies and the U.S. Census Bureau estimate that around 30 million people in the United States change residences each year (Carrigan, 2025; ; see also U.S. Census Bureau, n.d.). Now, well after the worst pandemic in a hundred years, we see ongoing problems related to inflation, employment, and, in particular, a shortage of affordable housing in some of our most populous cities. Current housing problems have been exacerbated by fires and hurricanes as well. Simultaneously, throughout the nation, the eviction and foreclosure rates appear higher than usual (Casey & Rico, 2023). This all suggests that there will be even more movers than in previous years. Added to the economic drivers for moving is the contemporary fact that many urban workers learned to work from home. And so, many of these workers are choosing to relocate to Idaho, Wyoming, North Carolina, and other more rural areas because technology lets them do so. This, too, suggests that there might even be more movers than usual during the coming years. My concern is that many of these movers may have school-age children, all of whom become the "new kid on the block."

It has also been commonplace for families in our country to move because of large swings in the economic cycles that affect particular regions and states. We've had "rust belts" in Michigan and Ohio. We've had loss of family farms and the reduction in farm labor throughout the Midwest, both recently and in the Dust Bowl years. And, of course, there was also a huge Black migration to the North and to the West, in search of economic advancement and greater racial justice (Wilkerson, 2010). Children were a part of each wave of migration. So changing one's residence more frequently than in other developed nations seems baked into American life, and thus American children, more than others, have to deal with such disruptions to their lives.

Furthermore, in the farms that still remain in the United States, seasonal migrant workers are often needed. Strangely enough, these workers also have children! Many of these children move from school to school in the United States, as well as between U.S. schools and schools in their home country. Also contributing to high mobility rates in our nation are the economic and political upheavals that frequently occur elsewhere in the world. Suddenly, in some communities, our public schools find themselves with an influx of Iranians, Iraqis, Somalis, Venezuelans, or Afghanis—new kids to the nation, as well as to the block! Furthermore, immigrant children are likely to be poor. On the other hand, there are the educationally advantaged immigrants from China, Japan, India, Nigeria, and other nations, who come for a few years to work at American universities and companies. These international visitors frequently have children with them.

In sum, the new kid on many American blocks may be the child of a highly educated immigrant from Southeast Asia, the child of an impoverished inner-city family who was placed for a few weeks with an aunt or grandmother in a different part of the city, the child of a migrant, or the child of an international or domestic businessperson—perhaps an engineer or computer expert—transferred from one region of our globe to another. Whatever the circumstances, such moves are hard on kids. The children must face new neighborhoods, new friends, new schools, new teachers, and sometimes even a new language! These are all difficult-to-navigate circumstances, even for the most well-adjusted children.

PART 1: A HIGHLY MOBILE NATION

I grew up in the heart of a huge urban area and went to the same public school building from kindergarten through 9th grade. My daughter, however, went to six schools across those same 10 years of kindergarten to 9th grade. And in one of those, on her first day of school, she was treated poorly by her teacher, and that teacher's antipathy to my daughter was picked up by the other kids in that class. My daughter experienced a form of institutionalized cruelty, and although that was decades ago, *she remembers it distinctly,* and so do I.

Frequently, the only reliable support for kids during these difficult times is their parents. But parental sensitivity and nurturance are not always as strong in the midst of a move as it might be otherwise. Moves can be hard on *all* members of the family. I was more aware of this than some because I knew the research. I knew that kids who moved frequently and who did not have strong support from parents and their schools could have life-long problems: Some of these young people have both attempted and committed suicide more frequently than the general population. And more than expected numbers of such youth have engaged with substance abuse and participated in violent crime later on in life (Anderson et al., 2014; DeWit, 1998; Qin et al., 2009).

Certainly, the positive correlations between number of moves early in life and problems later in life may well be the result of family dynamics that precipitated many of the residential moves. Poverty, violence, divorce, job changes, and job loss all could affect the psychosocial outcomes of individuals later in life. Perhaps it is these precipitating familial factors, not just the raw numbers of residential moves, that have such deleterious effects on behavior later in life. But even with this caveat, there does exist a strong consensus that frequent residential moves, particularly for introverted children, can be quite traumatic.

So I wasn't about to let our family moves be inordinately difficult for my children. Each of them grew up with no visible scars from my having to move them around when they were young. (I think!)

In fact, the stress frequently caused by moves was even recognized in the Old Testament. Deuteronomy 10:19 reminds us that "You shall also love the stranger, for you were strangers in the land of Egypt." So recognition of the stress associated with a move is at least a few thousand years old. Nevertheless, many of the negative effects of a move on school-age children could be greatly mitigated if schools, and the broader society they are part of, recognized the need to do something proactive about it.

Administrators, Teachers, and Schools

Educators don't intend to be cruel but, pressed with other demands, the new kid on the block is too often seen as a source of difficulty, not a cause for celebration. I think often of the Central Park East School, run by the properly lauded educator Debbie Meier. On a visit to a 4th-grade class there, I saw, off on the side, an Asian girl engaged with a (likely) Hispanic boy. I asked, "What are you guys doing?" The boy explained that the girl arrived yesterday from China, and he was her guide for that afternoon. She was teaching him Mandarin while he taught her English. They were trading words. All the kids took turns during the first few weeks, welcoming her to the class, and teaching her where things were—food and restrooms being among the most important! The teacher and the class ensured that the new kid's competencies were made evident: She could speak Mandarin! They wanted her to be their teacher! A series of students were simply excused from the assigned curriculum for a few hours each day during the first few weeks of the new student's enrollment. How simple it was to dramatically lessen the possibility of trauma in a school designed to care for all of its new kids on the block!

I worry about the sensitivity to these issues by school board members (invariably the community stayers, not the folks who move a lot). I worry also about administrators (invariably those who value stable enrollment figures, not enrollment fluctuations), and I worry too about teachers (invariably struggling to keep up with the workload in their present teaching assignment and who see class size as important). All these usually decent folks sometimes seem to forget the moral issues pertaining to nurturance of the young that motivated their desire to be in education. We all need to face it: Stable, small-town America does not exist, and maybe it never did! I doubt if there ever was a very stable time for America, a nation of immigrants, always on the move to find a better life. We have been a nation of westward movers, looking for chances at reinvention and searching for employment opportunities. Perhaps the dream of a fictitious stable past allows too many educators to see the new kids on the block as an anomaly, not the constant reality that they have been throughout our country's history.

Unrealized by many of our citizens is that even in communities and school districts perceived of as "stable," there are likely to be many schools with 20–30% "churn," a measure of mobility. Churn rates of 20–30% mean that between one-fifth (20%) to almost one-third of the children (30%) who start out the school year leave that school and are replaced by other students who enter the school before the end of the school year. Many Wisconsin public schools have churn rates of 40% or more, contributing to teachers' nightmares! And many charter schools in Wisconsin have churn rates from 80% to 100%! In fact, the typical churn rate in charter schools, particularly for online charters, is usually many times the churn rate of the public schools (*Milwaukee Journal Sentinel,* 2018; see also Shelly, 2007).

Estimates are that 30% of the nation's poorest children have attended at least three different schools by 3rd grade, while only 10% of middle-class children around that age have a school-moving rate that high. Furthermore, compared to white children, Black children were found to be twice as likely to change schools frequently. So schools that serve poor and minoritized children are most likely serving neighborhoods that have the highest rates of residential mobility in their region. I always wonder if any one of the bureaucrats in the U.S. Department of Education and in our Congress understand that schools that serve the poor, with mobility rates of the kind I just described, are a part of the reason we have the achievement gap that all of us want to reduce or have disappear. Why would any sane secretary of education, or any state or federal legislator, think that more testing will solve America's educational problems? All that increased testing has ever done is to reveal, over and over again, that schools with highly mobile student populations are typically schools where students score poorly on tests. Duh!

Is anyone reading this essay shocked by such a finding? The only thing shocking to me is that we don't work on reducing residential mobility, a contributing and possibly a causal factor in the low academic performance of low-income kids. Instead, too often we blame teachers and schools for their failures to close the achievement gap. I'd actually be quite happy to join in the criticism of some low-achieving schools as soon as we get rid of the income gap, the residential housing gap, the medical care gap, and the like. I am so damn tired of blaming America's schools for the broader problems of American society (Berliner & Biddle, 1996).

America's problems, inevitably, become our public schools' problems. For example, many homeless families often live in the neighborhoods with high mobility rates. These families are even more mobile than the ordinary residential movers in those neighborhoods, placing an even greater burden on nearby schools and their teachers. For example, on a single night in January 2024, the U.S. Department of Housing and Urban Development estimated that 771,480 people were homeless, with about 150,000 of them being children. Many were in family groups, living on the street or in a car, or in another place not meant for human habitation (Henry et al., 2021). Children among the homeless are often enrolled in whatever school is nearby, and may, unknown to school personnel, be separated from their family for a time. These children frequently leave their nearby school, and then come back to it, in the same school year. Such children are among the most highly mobile members of a school community. It comes as no surprise that these children struggle with high rates of mental health problems—anxiety, depression, or withdrawal—compared to other school-age children (Harris, 2016). Teachers almost unanimously will say that the more students move, the greater the severity of the behavioral problems they note in their classrooms. All this is to say, mobility and homelessness make it hard for certain schools to produce high-performing students until, and unless, mobility is reduced to the same rates as found in the general school population. So many of what we call failing schools are society's failure to deal with homelessness, rather than the failure of our nation's educators!

An illustration of the magnitude of the problem was illustrated by a school in upstate New York that had a churn rate of more than 100% about a decade ago. New students were arriving, and old students were leaving, almost every day, often with no warning provided to the school's administrators. And then, complicating the matter further, some of the students who had left returned. In a particular classroom, only three of the students who started that year remained throughout the year, while others entered and left and were replaced by still newer students. Because of migration patterns among the farm workers whose children were in this school, some of the children came, and went, and came back again in the same year. One child in this school had been in seven different schools between kindergarten and 3rd grade. In schools with high mobility, instructional routines are disrupted, the pace of instruction slows down, and the design of the curriculum is driven by the needs of the movers rather than by those who stay. Administrative resources are diverted to incorporating new students and processing the records of students who leave. As can be expected, teacher morale often falls, and subsequent teacher mobility adds to the problems of student mobility. Any sense of community at such schools is all but destroyed.

Students who move three or more times between the ages of 4 and 7 are 20% less likely than nonmovers to graduate from high school, after controlling for other student characteristics. Tragically, students from more stable families who attend schools with high turnover rates suffer academically as well. Why would it be otherwise? It makes sense that if the low income residential mobility rate could be brought down to the middle-class mobility rate, the achievement gap between low- and middle-income students would drop significantly. Similarly, if the mobility rate of Black students were to equal that of white students, the achievement gap between these two groups might also be significantly less.

Clearly, both movers and the stayers pay a price for living in neighborhoods with high rates of residential mobility and/or homelessness. Mobility and homelessness increased, of course, during the nation's recent pandemic and the problems that many Americans had with paying their rent or mortgages. It is not surprising, therefore, that on tests of school achievement, learning loss in children due to school policies associated with COVID-19 have now been documented, and, unsurprisingly, there was less loss for the wealthy and greater losses for the poorer children (Annie E. Casey Foundation, 2024). But how much larger those losses are for the children in families that moved during these times is unknown.

PART 2: SCHOOL PRACTICES

You may have guessed by now that I have a pet peeve: I really don't like schools being blamed for problems created by our economic system. That has to stop! Opinion shapers need to understand that mobility and homelessness are not conducive to high rates of school achievement, as measured by standardized achievement test scores. But I am also upset that the school personnel I so often admire occasionally lose their humanity in the process of dealing with this issue. Imagine for a moment how tough it is to be the newest kid in the class.

Even the most mentally healthy, optimistic child cannot help but feel a little scared, lonely, and embarrassed on first entering a new class at the elementary level or going to many new classes per day, as occurs in the upper grades. You can see these kids the first day, especially the adolescents, scrunching in their chairs trying not to be noticed at all. Rightly so, they feel ignorant about the local school norms and expectations. The more impoverished and distressed the family, the more intense these feelings must be on the first day of class, at still another new school!

I have found schools staffed by people who are ordinarily quite caring but who manage, in spite of their basic goodness, to treat the arrival of the new student after the start of the school year as an annoyance. This has to stop. When the unmistakable antipathy of a whole group of adults is communicated to the new kid at the school, we have failed our moral obligations as educators. Too many of us smile at the new child, say nice things to the new child, help the new child and family with the many forms that accompany the students' entrance to the school and, simultaneously, communicate clearly to that child that they are making everybody work harder than usual. What kid can't read a phony smile? In ways that are not easy to put into words, in too many schools, the newcomer senses that they are not wanted in that school or classroom, or perhaps not even wanted in that community, as has been the experience of many immigrants.

What Can Be Done?

I witnessed one wonderfully humane and thoughtful elementary school principal demonstrate the kind of caring for the new student and for his own school staff that I wish I saw more of. I was interviewing this principal when a mother and her child walked in off the street and asked to see him. While I sat over in the corner, quietly waiting to continue my interview, the principal dutifully met with the parent and her child. He helped put them both at ease, explained the programs, assisted with forms, and told them he would see the child the next morning. The mother, however, wanted the child to stay at school. She had errands to run and had to report to her new employer later that day. She angrily insisted that the school keep her child.

The principal, however, with a policy and a plan for bringing new children into the school, gently explained that he had moved a lot when he was young, and he always remembered that being a new kid in class was hard on him. Some of his teachers had similar experiences and so they all tried to make it easier for new children coming into this school. If he just walked over to a teacher with that child and said here's another new one, the child would recognize and possibly even hear the anger the teacher might express about being caught unaware, or being overloaded already. There would be no desk for the child. There would be no books for the child. The teacher would not have prepared the other children to welcome the new child, and it was important that the whole class be ready to make the new child feel welcome—to know their name, to pronounce it correctly, to get a "buddy" prepared to be the child's special guide for the first day, and to prepare others to be guides later in the week. Furthermore, this principal continued, the teachers in that grade needed to discuss which of them might best be able to serve that child's needs given the information obtained in the intake interview.

As the principal escorted the embarrassed mother to the door, I remembered again why I loved to work in education! Somebody has to care, *really* care, for the young in our complex world. And sometimes, in our public schools, ignored by the media, I stumble on those kinds of people. This principal was that kind of person. He saw a problem that both the new kids and his staff had, and it was solved in a humane way.

Are other schools reacting to this fact of contemporary American life in similarly humane ways? I hope so. But I fear that too many school districts or local schools have either no policy for welcoming new students, or a strictly bureaucratic one. Wouldn't we do better to have the principal and teaching staff ready in 24 hours to teach every new kid, rich or poor, white or non-white, the ways of that new school? Each new school is really like a new culture to be learned. And for some of the new kids—immigrants in particular—the task is harder because they might be learning a new culture and a new language simultaneously. And schools really do have their own culture and their own special language! They have SATs and ITBSs; resource rooms and multipurpose rooms; learning-disabled students and Limited English Proficient students, the LD and LEP kids. There are also "math facts" stations and reading corners, one set of rules for participating in social studies and a different set of rules for participating in mathematics, and so forth.

To learn the school culture and its language, every new kid ought to be assigned a "buddy." The buddy, a native of the school culture, is the informant to help the new kid learn such monumentally important things like the rules for going to the bathroom and, especially, where it is located! New kids need to be taught where, when, what, and how to eat; what the teacher likes or gets mad at; and so forth. Margaret Mead and other anthropologists would have learned nothing without a native to teach them the rules of the society they hoped to study. And let us be clear, each classroom is a micro-society, so each requires an informant, a buddy for its new kids. Classrooms in modern, highly mobile America must learn to celebrate the arrival of each new child; one single day of *not* belonging to a community is much too long a time for the new kid on the block to wait.

Besides teachers and school administrators, there are others who should think about the meaning of high mobility rates among school children, and ways that such children and their families can be helped. The federal government, the National Governors Association, and the Council of Chief State School Officers might all want to be sure that a confidential but computerized national school record system is working well, so pertinent files on a student could be accessed on the day that a child shows up at their new school. It is dismaying that a school trying to help place a new student must send for the old records, perhaps across the country, and then wait some time to receive them—if they come at all—even if they are computerized!

Even in our computerized age, school computer systems are rarely kept up as well as they might be at a for-profit corporation, where files between divisions can often be transferred instantaneously. So transferring computerized information about students is sometimes problematic. And, to further complicate this situation, the transfer of school records may be forbidden by laws that see the passing of such information as a violation of privacy laws.

Savvy parents bring records from their child's previous school with them. But not every parent knows to do this.

Further, it's often perceived as a costly imposition for the child's old school to send their files to the child's new school, particularly if the sending school feels that they have no obligation to that child or that family anymore. So requests for information about the new student's reading and language ability, talents and difficulties, inoculations and special needs often end up buried in a pile of materials that gets copied when someone in a fiscally strapped district has the time to run all that stuff off, assuming there is enough money in the copy budget!

While such a delay occurs, the teacher at the new school must make decisions immediately. And this can result in (a) the new kid receiving instruction that they already have had, or (b) providing the new kid with instruction for which they are not prepared. What an awful way to run the systems that purport to value America's youth!

I was discouraged to learn that even across cities, sometimes within the same school district, the records for the new kid can take a week or more to get to the child's new school. This is all the more troublesome because these are the kinds of problems that are easily fixed. We may not know how to transform poor learners into college graduates or how to break the cycle of poverty in our inner cities. But I really do know how to get computer records transferred from one school to another school in 24 hours. Not to do so is negligent, mean-spirited, and uncaring of our youth; it undermines the professionalism we hope to see in all our educational systems.

And while trying to embarrass some of our school leaders by this tirade of mine, I might as well mention still another gripe that I have about big-city schools and the ways they have responded to the issue of high student mobility. For low-income families, a great deal of the mobility that we see is *within* the same district. A child might move to his grandmother's residence, then back with his family, then the family moves to another part of town, then the child goes back to Mexico, Puerto Rico, or Appalachia for a few weeks, then comes back and the family gets another apartment requiring registration at yet another school, and so forth. In some school districts, the curriculum materials encountered by young students at each school within the same district may be different.

Perhaps this occurs because of an interest in granting academic freedom for teachers and schools. That's not a bad idea. Perhaps this occurs because of a desire to decentralize authority. That, too, is not a bad idea. But perhaps this occurs because of a simple lack of thought. The result is that inner-city youngsters with the most severe learning needs will sometimes have to confront new curriculum materials once, twice, sometimes even three times each year. They can bounce from phonics to whole language, or they may bounce from materials that are like programmed instruction, to computer-assisted reading programs. They may go from the mathematics texts of Ginn Publishers to those of Houghton Mifflin, or to Scott Foresman, or to McGraw Hill. That's nonsense. It is indisputably in the best interest of the most mobile group of children that a school district agrees on a single series of curriculum materials for its students. This is particularly true for those whose skills are not yet too advanced, say those in the first four or five grades. It is not fair to subject the new kids in the school to these additional educational problems as they move from school to school within the same district. Allowing some semblance of site-based management is a great thing. Some school autonomy, some school-based decision-making is certainly laudable. But it can be a hurdle for the kids who are moving a lot if it entails encountering different curriculum materials at the same grade, in different schools, in the same district. Surely the teachers in a school district could agree on a standard curriculum for the first few grades, using the same set of texts, promoting the same learning experiences, and testing the same kinds of learning experiences, to make the problems of moving in our highly mobile society no harder on our youngest students then it need be.

CONCLUSION

What I'd like is for every school in America to recognize the changes in our ways of living and to develop policies that could make life a little easier for all the new kids on the block. A school never teaches just content, and the content that they do teach may be the last thing a child will remember about a particular school. *Schools are remembered by their humaneness or their antipathy in dealing with children and their families.* And those features of a school get communicated on the very first day a child enters school, by everyone already at that school—its students, janitors, cafeteria workers, and school secretaries, as well as its administrators and teachers. Anything less than a welcoming environment for the new kid is not merely unprofessional, it is heartless.

The Great Switcheroo

The academic and social competencies of the children who enter a school play a big role in determining the achievement test scores of students at that school. That is a fact. If you doubt that school achievement test scores are strongly influenced by the makeup of the student population of a school, you have not paid attention to the writing on poverty and achievement over the past few centuries! Teacher quality, facility quality, budget, leadership, textbooks, all play a role in achievement test scores—but none is more influential than the home lives of a school's children.

But I am convinced there has been a concerted effort to deny this well-established fact. A few decades ago, a change took place in the way we, the American public, think about education. We were systematically led by political leaders of both parties, but particularly Republicans, to ignore the *inputs* to our schools, by which I mean the characteristics of the students in the schools. Instead, we have been led to concentrate on the *outputs* of our schools, including student test scores, graduation rates, college attendance rates, and so forth. Every other input/output model I know of requires keeping a sharp eye on both. That is because *the inputs to a system are almost always related to the outputs of that system*. Duh!

I call what happened the Great Switcheroo; America's attention was diverted from broad issues of poverty and thus diverted from concerns about housing, food insecurity, medical treatment, single-parent families, crime, drug use, lack of role models, a stagnant minimum wage, and the like. Instead, attention was focused on issues related to the outputs and characteristics of schooling: test scores, teacher tenure, unionization, teacher incompetence, and the magically always wonderful alternatives to our allegedly "failing" public schools, namely, publicly supported voucher and charter schools. The Great Switcheroo meant that both news media and elected officials would come to focus on school achievement, college readiness, and competitiveness with China or Japan, rather than pay attention to hunger, housing, medical assistance, or the failure of the minimum wage to keep families free of those stressors.

The Great Switcheroo took place quietly, hardly noticed, as America moved from concern about the *inputs* to our schools, to concern about the *outputs* of our schools. Educators certainly have known for decades, if not centuries, that the fiscal and intellectual poverty of families affects the achievement of students in a nation's schools. But our nation—particularly Republican leaders, and with the concurrence of many Democrats—decided it did not want to fix the problems of poverty and its sequelae. Instead, they not only blamed virtually all the problems of academic achievement on our schools, they put the responsibility for curing those particular problems on the schools!

My colleague Jim Crawford (2006) provided some of the documentation for the Great Switcheroo. He found, for example, that from 1981 to 1990 the *New York Times* archives held 86 articles on Equal Educational Opportunity (EEO)—almost 10 per year. Writers concerned with EEO focused on the *inputs* to our schools, frequently focusing on remediation for the effects of poverty on school achievement. This was, in part, the legacy of Lyndon Johnson's presidency (1963–1969). It was Johnson who tried to lead us into a "war on poverty." Instead, our nation became mired in a war on the Vietnamese. But before Johnson ever served in Congress, let alone as president, he was a public school teacher. He knew, as every teacher knows, the relationship of inputs to outputs, and the powerful influence that the former has on the latter. More colloquially, and in the language that Lyndon Johnson frequently used—poverty sucks!

Looking now at the year 2007, during the presidency of George W. Bush (2001–2009), there were only three articles published by the *New York Times* about Equal Educational Opportunity. EEO had dropped off the nation's radar screen.

But did something replace EEO as a concern for our nation's schools, or did it just fade away as a national or newsworthy concern? Actually, it had already been replaced—a switch had occurred. The Great Switcheroo had gone almost unnoticed.

Equal Educational Opportunity as an educational goal was replaced by the pursuit of ever-higher test scores as our national educational goal. In 2007, when EEO seems to have disappeared, the *New York Times* published 35 articles on the achievement gap. So in the nation's most prestigious newspaper, in its reporting on education, the object of attention had turned from inputs to outputs.

The number of articles on outputs of the educational system published that year, compared to articles that were focused on inputs to the system, was 35 to 3! About a 12 to 1 ratio. But it wasn't just the *Times*: A change in the ratio of the number of articles published on EEO versus poor test scores was about the same in the *Washington Post,* the *Los Angeles Times,* the *Boston Globe,* and the *Chicago Tribune.* In short, the most prestigious and well-read newspapers in the United States, newspapers that were trusted by millions, had silently pulled off the Great Switcheroo. Concern about inputs to our schools was replaced by concerns for the outputs of our schools, basically ignoring the obvious relationship between the two.

In particular, during the George W. Bush presidency, our government pushed their No Child Left Behind plan. The Bush administration, following the lead of the Reagan administration, pushed the idea that American public schools were not good. They attributed the dysfunction that they perceived to a lack of school accountability, particularly to the poor quality of America's teachers. The numbers of folks in poverty—in all of poverty's many manifestations—appeared too difficult a problem for Republican administrations to address. Teacher fecklessness was an easier argument to make.

Perhaps an attack on teachers was substituted for an attack on poverty because Republicans regularly seek to lower taxes. Thus, they are loathe to facilitate programs that might alleviate poverty or its effects because—surprise, surprise—*such programs require government funding.* On the other hand, attacking teachers can be done for free!

What actually was needed was money to address poverty. Much less helpful were the lectures by Republicans on "responsibility," and their yearning to keep government out of the lives of our citizens—even when some of our citizens were frequently hungry, unsheltered, and without medical care! Republicans in general saw no reason to spend tax revenues on alleviating the effects of the myriad variables correlated with poverty. That the fiscal cost was too high—and the inane philosophical belief that each person should pull themselves up by their own bootstraps even if they have no shoes—was the dominant theme of Republicanism at that time. They didn't want to pay the fiscal or philosophical costs of helping with food insecurity, single-parent households, frequent household moves, inadequate medical care, lack of vocational training and retraining, drug use, or lack of adequate transportation. An unspoken piece of the defense of these (mostly) Republican positions was racism—since recipients of funding for poverty-related issues were disproportionately people of color.

So instead of dealing with poverty, it was bad teachers, bad curriculum, bad administrators, inadequate parents, and the like that were all offered as the reason that some students and some schools did not achieve as much as Republican administrations and most other Americans desired. To accept the alternative, namely, that poverty and its correlates were the primary reason for many children not doing as well in schools as society desired, means that a partial solution to our concerns for higher school achievement might be possible. But the costs to alleviate poverty, in the richest country the world had ever known, was considered too much of a burden, and also philosophically unwise. It is likely, the argument went, that expenditures of this type would just breed more of the "welfare queens" that Reagan was always complaining about, but had trouble finding.

- Perhaps more support for unionization might help alleviate poverty.
- Perhaps a decent minimum wage that kept up with inflation might help alleviate poverty.
- Perhaps better health care and prescription drug coverage for all might help alleviate poverty.
- Perhaps better child care for working mothers might help alleviate poverty.
- Perhaps rental assistance and facility inspections might help to provide stable living conditions for families and thus help alleviate poverty.

But those solutions rarely get much of an airing in Republican-controlled states, and only rarely does Congress take up similar matters, even today. So if solutions like those just noted are off the table, how else might we combat the effects of poverty on school achievement? More simply put, how can our schools be fixed for as little of an investment of tax dollars as possible?

The Bush administration decided that the solution was to go after lazy and inadequate schoolteachers, as well as their inept school administrators and their protective unions. The culprits for low achievement test scores had been found! It wasn't poverty—everyone could point to a poor boy or girl who had made it to the top of the income bracket. Rags to riches was the American dream, and it certainly has happened. So it must be possible for *everyone* except those whom the administration blamed for their own poverty: the lazy, the welfare queens, the drug-using, pot-smoking families, all of whom had been given the gift of God, citizenship in the U.S. of A.

So clearly poverty wasn't the obstacle to great achievements! The Bush administration, through its Department of Education, was going to force those lazy American children, and their lazy American teachers, to start producing higher test scores . . . or else! Poverty was out and test scores were in as the object of concern.

Nowhere was this Switcheroo more obvious than on the White House website: During the Bush years there were 344 documents concerned with the achievement gap (outputs), while there were only three documents concerned with equal educational opportunity (inputs). Remedies for poor school performance were sought by studying the outputs rather than the inputs to the system, at a ratio of 344 to 3! The Great Switcheroo had been made, and it was used to make policy by the next president's choice of an educational leader, the absolute educational numbskull Arne Duncan.

A wrong-headed concentration on outputs is actually easy to understand. Our youth are in classrooms, so when those classrooms do not function as we want them to, we go to work on improving them—new curriculum, computer-based learning, and lots of assessments. Those class-rooms are in schools, so when we decide that those schools are not perform-ing appropriately, we go to work on improving them as well. We authorize charter schools and provide vouchers for private schools as alternatives to the schools that we judge to be failing, or we close down schools and redis-tribute their students. But it is an act of great ignorance to forget, or pur-posely ignore, the obvious reality that both students and schools are situated in neighborhoods filled with families, many of whom are poor. Those poor are not a random cross-section of Americans. There is huge overrepresenta-tion of some groups and not others among the poor. All of America's neigh-borhoods are highly segregated by social class, race, ethnicity, immigration status, crime rates, and so forth. This reality has always led me to believe that every one of the myriad school-based solutions designed to improve achievement in schools that are not scoring well on assessments was likely to be inadequate. What happens in so many schools trying to do better is much too easily affected by, perhaps even negated by, neighborhood and family norms, and by family hardships.

Here it is, folks, a truth we cannot escape: What happens outside of school has a huge impact on what happens inside a school (see Figure 10.1). Republican administrations in general, and G. W. Bush's administration in particular, refused to recognize that.

Some of that negativity toward our schools carried over into the Obama administration. And in the Trump administration that followed, the blame was clearly pointed at teachers and school administrators, not poverty or the social conditions accompanying poverty. In fact, in his ghost-written book *The America We Deserve* (2000), President Trump actually made this

Figure 10.1. Blaming Schools Unfairly

Artist: Monte Wolverton. Source: Used with permission from www.CartoonStock.com.

enormously stupid and patently untrue statement, in support of the "output" wing of the Republican party:

> According to school-testing experts' rule of thumb, the average child's achievement score *declines* about 1 percent for each year they're in school. . . .

In my many years of hanging around experts in education and in assessment, I never heard of one dumb enough to say that! Only Trump was stupid enough to say, and perhaps believe, that.

I am sure that improving classrooms and schools, working on curricula and standards, improving teacher quality, and fostering better use of technology in classroms are certainly helpful. But sadly, such activities may also be similar to those of the drunk found on his hands and knees under a streetlamp. When asked by a passerby what he was doing, the drunk replied that he was looking for his keys. When asked where he lost them, the drunk replied, "over there," and pointed back up the dark street. When the passerby then asked the drunk why he was looking for the keys where they were standing, the drunk answered, "the light is better here!"

We need to understand that the more important keys to educational reform are up the block, in the shadows, where the light is not as bright. If we do choose to peer into the dark, we might see what the late eminent sociologist Elizabeth Cohen saw quite clearly: That poverty constitutes the unexamined 600-pound gorilla that *most* affects American education (see Figure 10.2, below). I am convinced that this country will never have the kind of overall school achievement it desires if we don't address our American gorilla.

The economist Richard Rothstein (2004) understands this quite well. He noted that policymakers almost always conclude that the existing and persisting achievement gaps we see, both within and between schools, must be

Figure 10.2. The 600-Pound Gorilla in the Classroom

the result of erroneous school policies. Those who blame America's schools believe that teachers' expectations are too low, teachers are not sufficiently qualified, or that curricula are inappropriate, leadership is unfocused, and schools are way too undisciplined. School critics often believe some, or all, of these factors! Sadly, too many Americans conclude that the root of the achievement gap is in its "failing schools," not its distressed neighborhoods or families. While that makes the most sense to many people it is completely wrong and it is also, simultaneously, heartless.

I bring the gorilla, representing poverty, to our attention to remind us all that education doesn't only take place in our schools, a point that Pulitzer Prize–winning historian Lawrence Cremin (1989) tried to make as the school reform movement gained momentum in the late 1980s, when our nation was afraid that the Japanese were about to overtake, if not destroy, America's economic system. Cremin noted that in contemporary American life too many of the poorest of the children who entered our schools had spent no time at all in school-like settings during the first 5 years of their life. The situation is better now because Head Start and other subsidized early childhood programs make a difference, but still, a limited percentage of 3- and 4-year-olds from poor backgrounds attend preschool. But here is the even bigger issue: When these children reach school age, they only spend about 30 of their waking hours a week in our schools, and they do this only for about two-thirds of the weeks in a year. You can do the arithmetic that follows yourself.

In the course of a full year, separate from sleep time, students might spend somewhere around 1,000 hours in school, and close to 5,000 hours in their neighborhood and with their families. For all youth, those 5,000 hours require learning to be a member of one or more cultural groups in their community, learning to behave appropriately in diverse settings, learning ways to get along with others, to fix things, to think about the world they were brought into, as well as to explain things to others, to play on teams, and so forth. These are natural and influential experiences in growing up. But for poor kids, what is learned in those settings can often be unhelpful, and too often, harmful.

It was Jean Anyon (1997), among others, who some time ago alerted us to the fact that many of the families in impoverished neighborhoods are poorly equipped to raise healthy children, that the schools those children attend would have a hard time educating them, even if those schools were well organized and run, and had access to extra resources. And while there do exist schools for poor kids that are excellent, in way too many poor neighborhoods, they are not. Compared to schools serving wealthier kids, schools serving poor kids often have higher teacher turnover, more teacher shortages, teachers with lower qualifications, higher student absenteeism, and equipment and school buildings that need repair. Anyon said that it had become increasingly clear by the end of the 20th century that several decades of educational reform had not brought substantial improvements to America's inner cities. And the cause of that, she thought, was that most school reform efforts did not take into account the social context of poverty and race in which inner-city schools are located. They focused on outputs, not inputs, having bought into the Great Switcheroo. It continues today, over 2 decades into the 21st century.

Anyon pointed out that even the best educational reforms cannot really compensate for the ravages of society. She said: "Attempting to fix inner-city schools without fixing the city in which they are embedded, is like trying to clean the air on one side of a screen door." I am not sure it can be said any better!

The real failure in inner-city schools, she noted, is political, economic, and cultural, rather than bad teachers or administrators. It is these factors—politics, economics, and culture—that must be changed before meaningful school improvement projects can be successfully implemented.

As educators and scholars, we continually talk about school reform as if it must take place inside the schools, downplaying the role of the world the students inhabit outside of school. So we advocate frequently for adequacy in funding, high-quality teachers, professional development, greater subject-matter preparation, cooperative learning, technologically enhanced instruction, community involvement, and lots of other ideas and methods that I am happy to also promote. Some of the most lauded of our school reform programs in our most distressed schools do show some success, but success often means bringing the skills of the students who are at the 20th percentile in reading and mathematics up to the 30th percentile. A school reform effort that raises achievement 10% for a whole school is certainly worthy of our admiration, but it just doesn't get as much accomplished as needs to be.

We are not doing enough to change educational achievement in our nation because our vision of how to improve student achievement is so limited. It is limited by our collective views about the proper and improper roles of government in ameliorating the problems that confront us in our schools; our beliefs about the ways in which a market economy is supposed to work; our concerns about what constitutes appropriate tax rates for the nation; our religious views about the elect and the damned; our structural racism and social class prejudices; our peculiar American ethos of individualism; and our almost absurd belief that schooling is the cure for whatever ails society. These well-entrenched views that we hold as a people make helping the poor seem like some kind of communist or atheistic plot! And it makes one an apostate in reference to the myth about the power of the public schools to affect change.

James Traub (2000), writing in the *New York Times*, said this all, quite well, many years ago. He noted that it was hard to think of a more satisfying solution to poverty than education. Compared to other suggestions for alleviating poverty in America, investments in school reform really involve relatively little money out of the huge federal and state budgets we allocate for education across our nation. So relying on the schools to alleviate poverty asks practically nothing of the non-poor, who typically control our society's resources. Traub also noted that depending on school reform to alleviate poverty is related to the great American myth of individualism. The poor, through our public schools, get a chance to pull themselves up by their own bootstraps. It's the American way!

Furthermore, the idea that schools cannot cure poverty by themselves sounds something like a vote of no confidence in our great American capacity for self-transformation. The Horatio Alger myth—attainment of riches through hard work, honesty, and a little luck—is a part of the American story. Moreover, if our public schools seem unable to transform its poorest students into middle-class or occasionally wealthy adults, we end up also flirting with racial theories suggesting that educational inequality has its roots in biological inequality (Herrnstein & Murray, 1994).

But an alternative explanation to the idea that poor families are biologically determined is that educational inequality is rooted in economic problems and social pathologies that are simply too deep to be overcome by school alone. And if that's true, as Rothstein, Cremin, Anyon, Traub, and I believe, then there really is every reason to think about the limits of schooling as the great equalizer, the great balance wheel of society, as Horace Mann once declared.

So here it is now—the focus of this entire essay: *Schooling alone may be too weak an intervention for improving the lives of most children now living in poverty.* Those who blame poor children and their families for their lack of success in school, citing their behavior or their genes, or those who blame the teachers and administrators who serve those kids and families through our public schools, are all refusing to acknowledge the root problem faced by too many American schools, namely, that there is a 600-pound gorilla in the schoolhouse with them!

Poverty is the biggest educational issue for Americans to deal with. And while the poor may always be with us, do we really need to accept that having so many poor children in our country is just the way it is? A recent report of the Organisation for Economic Co-operation and Development (OECD) (2021) estimates that the poverty rate for children under 17 years of age in Finland is about 4%; in Denmark and Iceland it is about 5%; in Norway and Sweden it is 8–9%; in Hungary and Belgium it is about 10%. The United States, the richest country in the world, has a poverty rate for children under age 17 of over 21%! This ought to be shameful . . . but apparently it is not.

We need more of our leaders to look at Table 10.1 (see Ratcliffe, 2015), with its simple message about poverty and its relationship to some life outcomes. Kids who grow up in poverty cost us lots more as adults than do kids

Table 10.1. School and Life Outcomes

	Never Been Poor Growing Up	Experienced Poverty When Growing Up
Receives high school diploma by age 20	92.7%	77.9%
Enrolls in postsecondary course work by age 25	69.7%	41.4%
Completes college by age 25	36.5%	13.0%
Is consistently employed between ages 25–30	70.3%	57.3%
Is not associated with a premarital teen birth	96.0%	78.0%
Never arrested by age 20	84.2%	76.3%

who do not grow up in poverty. The message seems clear: Fix it now, or pay later, when it is likely to be a lot more expensive!

This essay on the pernicious effects of poverty on our society is not intended to deny the power of individual educators and schools to influence individual students in positive ways. That happens all the time. And we certainly should more frequently honor those teachers and administrators who do change the lives of our students into something better than what might be predicted for them from their residence in impoverished neighborhoods, and their membership in dysfunctional families. Jonathan Kozol, after many years of describing the debilitating effects of poverty, also wrote *Fire in the Ashes* (2013). Here he wrote about the power of teachers, families, clergy, social workers, and others as they helped children overcome the myriad negative factors associated with poverty in America. Despite the ashes, some fire was still burning, and when kindled, successful lives were still possible to achieve.

We know this, but we encounter America's youth primarily in our public schools, and forget the importance of their families and neighborhoods. For example, the correlation of income between siblings in the Nordic countries is around .20, indicating that only about 4% of the variance in the incomes of siblings could be attributable to joint family influences (Björklund et al., 2002). But in the United States the correlation between the income of siblings is over .40, indicating that about 16% of the variance among incomes of siblings in the United States is due to family. This makes the Nordic countries appear to be much more meritocratic than the United States.

Family, for good or for bad, exerts 4 times the influence on income earned by siblings in the United States than in the Nordic countries. Sibling income also provides evidence that class lines in the United States are harder to overcome today than previously (Levine & Mazumder, 2003). In fact, sibling incomes have grown quite a bit closer in the United States over the last few decades, indicating that family resources (or the lack of them) play an increasing role in one's success in life. At least one reason for that is the increasingly unequal schooling provided to our nation's middle- and lower-class children.

But an alternative explanation to Herrnstein and Murray "is that educational inequality is rooted in economic problems and social pathologies too deep to be overcome by school alone. And if that's true, then there really is every reason to think about the limits of school" (Traub, 2000, p. 54).

J'Accuse

Too Many of Arizona's Politicians Have Been Mean, Cheap, Undemocratic, and On the Dole

I left Arizona recently. But I haven't forgotten my obligation to speak out about educators and education in a state I spent many happy years trying to improve. And while it is not pleasant to believe, sadly, I really do think that many of the people we elected to make Arizona a great place in which to live have been mean, cheap, undemocratic, and doing the bidding of influential out-of-state contributors to their reelection campaigns. Regrettably, what is happening in Arizona infects many states across America. I am afraid that many readers will see that this is so.

Consider my claim of meanness. High-quality early childhood education is not universal in Arizona. It is, however, provided for many of the children of wealthier and better-educated families, but such an experience would certainly be of greater benefit to the children of the middle class and poor. A host of respected researchers inform us that high-quality early education programs frequently produce the following outcomes:

1. Substantially reduced numbers of children identified as needing special education, with a resultant reduction in school costs;
2. A much-reduced achievement gap between children in the lowest and highest social classes (that is good for democracy);
3. Reduced health problems throughout individuals' lives (that is both a humane outcome and reduces society's costs for health care);
4. Reduced dropout rates in high school (that has future tax savings for a community);
5. Increased high school graduation rates (that also has future tax savings for a community);
6. Higher college attendance rates after high school (that benefits local businesses);
7. Higher employment rates after high school (that increase tax revenues);
8. Lower incarceration rates as adults (that lowers the costs to the community and state, as well as avoids the personal tragedies for families); and

9. Over about 30 years, high-quality early education provides a return on investment approaching 10%.

So if you live in a community with many poor children, and you expect that community to still be around 30 years later, it is foolish, *perhaps mean-spirited*, not to invest in high-quality early childhood education.

But what about costs? Yes, there is that. Universal high-quality early childhood education programs are not cheap. However, economists estimate that Arizona's return on investment when supporting early childhood education will approach 10%. A 10% rate of return, though well into the future, is pretty darn good! So not to support universal high-quality early education is mean, cheap, and foolish. An embarrassing accusation!

My state of Arizona demonstrated that its politicians are cheap and mean in other ways. For example, although the state seems to worry a lot about undocumented individuals in the abstract, it doesn't worry at all about documentation for the teachers of the state's poorest citizens. Some time ago, the state's chief executive at the time, Governor Ducey, signed SB1042 so that school districts having difficulties hiring trained educators with classroom experience can, instead, hire people who want to teach but do not have any formal training. And they do not even need a bachelor's degree if they have worked in a related field.

This led me to think about other ways the governor could help Arizonans thrive. For example, it is well known that rural emergency rooms have shortages of well-trained personnel. And it just happens that I have always found surgery fascinating and my hand is still steady as a rock. I also have experience dissecting frogs, although that was a while back. Furthermore, I do indeed hold a doctor's degree, in fact I have three of them, albeit none in medicine. But, heck, one doctoral degree is probably as good as another, and I have three! If needed, I am available weekends to do surgery.

Arizona's legislation shows how amazingly disrespectful the legislature and governor are of teachers, thinking that no particular knowledge or skill is really needed to be a teacher. Has no one ever told our political leaders that typical district employees who come into teaching through these alternative routes leave the field at incredibly high rates in their first year or two? That Teach for America (TFA) teachers, with little or no training, who came to work in Arizona classrooms that served poor kids also break their contracts at a high rate as soon as they find out how hard it is to be a teacher (Veltri, 2010).

I have heard Arizona legislators remark that they didn't think teaching was really so hard. Heck, they said, they taught their kids and their dogs all sorts of things, so how hard can it be to teach what schools try to teach? What these politicians don't know is that one set of researchers established that classroom teachers may, at a minimum, make 42 consequential decisions per hour, 252 per day! Other researchers say the number of consequential decisions is between 1,200–1,800 a day, almost all of which are unplanned and unpredictable. *Classroom teaching, therefore, is enormously complex and requires exhausting cognitive and emotional work.* This is what the dilettantes who want to teach and the TFA volunteers find out quite quickly. So Arizona's legislation to fill classrooms with unqualified teachers—sometimes called scabs, in similar circumstances—does nothing to solve the problem in the long term.

Our politicians do not understand that solid research informs us that teachers do not achieve their best in terms of improving their students' test scores until they have about 10 years of teaching under their belts. So, if you cannot keep teachers in classrooms and schools, you never will see the teachers you hire at their best. Surely, all politicians know that "churn"— the rapid turnover of employees in any organization—will ensure that the organization will never function at its highest effectiveness. High churn rates for teachers are no different.

As a general rule, the greater the churn rate, the lower a school will score on standardized achievement tests. Teacher communities of caring and professionalism—so common in successful schools—never form when teacher churn rates are high. Furthermore, don't these politicians understand that replacing teachers who quit can often cost $20,000 or more per occurrence, although that cost is partially offset by offering the replacement a lower salary? Thus, reducing churn rates by paying teachers decently, as well as honoring those who teach, actually can moderate districts' costs while increasing a district's academic performance.

Maybe legislators are merely ignorant. I've certainly met some who are. But I am afraid I cannot shake my belief that it is much more likely that they are cheap and mean. I wonder if there is a single legislator in Arizona, or in the rest of the nation, who would reject this idea: "If you pay enough, you can almost always find talented people to staff any position!" Want someone beaten up or murdered? Pay enough and it can happen! In fact, it happens all the time! Don't trust my opinion? I'm from the Bronx! Want help in dumping a terrible spouse? Pay lawyers enough and that, too, can happen. If you want a great new CEO for your company, pay enough and you probably will find one. Want the finest surgeon in the world? Pay the fee!

And what if we want a decent 3rd-grade teacher who will make a career out of public school teaching? Oh, sorry, "We can't seem to find one of those anywhere!" So, instead, let's let unlicensed, possibly poorly educated, certainly unprepared dilettantes into America's classrooms, and pay them as little as we pay the professionals who ordinarily staff our schools, knowing full well that one reason the opening for a teacher exists is because we do not pay teachers enough! Cheap, cheap, cheap is all that comes to mind! Arizona's pay scale for teachers and its funding for schools puts the political and educational leaders of the state I worked in clearly on record as not wanting the best for its children. It wants the cheapest caretaking it can get. Most Arizona legislators seem to have no shame about underpaying talented teachers for the work they do.

Sadly, I think I have supported the charge that our legislators are mean and cheap, at least in some of the domains over which they have oversight. But I cannot help adding one more example of pure meanness by Arizona's leaders. This is Arizona's use of the A–F grading system for the public schools of the state, based on a school's standardized test scores, a practice all too frequently repeated across the country. Let me be clear: Almost the entire research community is in agreement that the amount of variation that we see in standardized test scores that can be attributed to the teachers or the school itself is trivial. The variation in test scores between schools—which is certainly large—is overwhelmingly accounted for by the demographics of the families attending the school, as well as the characteristics of the neighborhoods from which a school draws its students.

"A" and "B" schools, with very rare exceptions, are schools for the wealthy, and the "D" and "F" schools are schools for the poor. The A and B schools in Arizona typically have populations heavily weighted toward white middle-class kids, while the D and F schools typically have more poor kids, particularly Hispanics, with many English learners among them. In other words, Arizona's school letter grades, with few exceptions, are income-based, correlating strongly with median household income and median home prices in the catchment area of the school. Because of this, school letter grades are misleading, if not stupid, because they reflect demographics rather than the quality of education offered by the school. They are used primarily by politicians and Realtors.

To accurately judge the quality of education that occurs in a school would probably require about a half-dozen visits to the school by at least half a dozen knowledgeable professionals, and that costs a lot of money, so it is virtually never done. Instead, politicians choose to use standardized test scores to judge school professionals' quality, even if those tests are completely invalid for that purpose. This implies that Arizona's legislators are surely ignorant about the concept of test validity. But mean is still a part of this story.

In Arizona, each school that receives letter ratings must then send a letter out to all the parents and business leaders of the school's catchment area informing them of their school rating. For the schools that receive Ds and Fs, this is a shaming process that blames hard-working teachers and administrators for the poverty of the children they teach. That's the mean part. Instead of medals for their good work with children and families in poverty, teachers and administrators are shamed because of the test scores that arise from the poverty in their communities.

Moreover, those school letter ratings have at least two side effects: First, those school ratings immediately raise or lower housing prices in the school area, making poorer districts poorer and making richer districts richer, contributing to increased segregation between different socioeconomic levels. The school grades, which have nothing to do with the quality of schooling, teaching, or learning, and everything to do with family income, inevitably contribute to the development of an apartheid-lite system of schooling.

Yes, apartheid-lite is the right term for housing that concentrates poor, often minoritized children in specific neighborhoods based on income—not race or ethnicity, because that would be illegal. The legislative demand that letters be sent informing a community of the letter grades received by their local schools is the mean part. It makes teachers the villains in a society that has found ways to segregate families by income. This shaming of teachers and administrators has caused some of those whom I admire to quit the profession. A loss we should not have to suffer, were it not for a mean legislature.

I loved my 50 or so years working in Arizona, and I still care deeply about the education of youth in the state I called home for so many years. I am particularly concerned about the environment found by our newest immigrants to Arizona, many of whom are poor and not English-speaking. Some recent elections in Arizona give me hope that those elected to office will be less mean and less frugal than have the politicans of the past, and will try harder to support the educational health and welfare of all Arizona's citizens. One recent election, although close, portends something new for Arizonans—a repudiation of the mean and cheap legislators who populated the state's past.

I am hopeful. I hope that in Arizona's future, as well as in our nation, that we see a more humane and caring system for its poorest citizens, and that we see, as well, more respect and more funding for its schools.

Why Religious Schools Should Never Receive a Dollar of Public Funding

I believe in the separation of church and state. I think it has done the United States a lot of good to honor Jefferson's metaphoric and aspirational "wall" between the two. I also believe that money corrupts too many people and too many institutions. Holding those two beliefs simultaneously means that (1) I never want to see any local, state, or federal money used to aid any religious group, and (2) I don't want to see any religious group, or affiliated religious organizations, donating to the campaigns of public officials. The latter may be impossible to stop in an era of dark money. But the former—government support of religious institutions—is almost always done in public view and is worth stopping now, immediately, as it could easily damage our fragile republic.

Overstated? Hardly! Read on! Few citizens pay attention to the expenditure of public dollars for the support of religious schools, but it occurs frequently. It can cost citizens billions of dollars annually, and ends up supporting some horrible things. A contemporary example of this is the criteria for entrance to the Fayetteville Christian School in North Carolina.

Fayetteville Christian School (FCS) were recipients, in a recent school year, of $495,966 of *public* money. They get this in the form of school vouchers that are used by students and their families to pay for the students' religious schooling. The entrance requirements for this school, and other religious schools like it, are quite frightening to me, though clearly acceptable to North Carolinians. From their website (www.fayettevillechristian.com), in 2020:

> The student and at least one parent with whom the student resides must be in agreement with (our) Statement of Faith and have received Jesus Christ as their Savior. In addition, the parent and student must regularly [go to] a local church. [We] will not admit families that belong to or express faith in religions that deny the absolute Deity/Trinity of Jesus Christ as the one and only Savior and path to salvation. . . . FCS will not admit families that engage in behaviors that Scripture defines as deviate and sin (illicit drug use, sexual promiscuity, homosexuality [LGBT], etc.).

Once admitted, if the student or parent/guardian with whom the student resides becomes involved in lifestyles contradictory to Biblical beliefs, we may choose to dis-enroll the student/family from the school.

So, despite the receipt of *public* money, the Fayetteville Christian School is really not open to the public at all! This school says, up front and clearly, that it doesn't want and will not accept Jews, Muslims, Hindus, and many others. Further, although supported by *public* money, it will expel students for their family's alleged "sins." Is papa smoking pot? Expelled! Does your sibling have a homosexual relationship? Out you go! Has mama filed for divorce? You are gone! The admissions and dismissal policies of this school—receiving about a half million dollars of *public* funds per year—are scandalous. I'd not give them a penny! North Carolina legislators, and the public who elects them, should all be embarrassed to ever say they are upholders of American democracy. They are not.

Beside the antidemocratic admission and retention problems in many religious schools, Christian or otherwise, some have serious curriculum problems as well. Those curriculum problems actually terrify me when they occur in publicly supported religious schools. With public money—*my money*—many of these schools spread ideas that are objectively/scientifically untrue. Furthermore, some of those ideas are repugnant!

Do you remember Bobby Jindal? A few years back, Jindal was governor of Louisiana and even, for a short time, a candidate for president of the United States of America. He pushed hard for publicly supported charter and voucher schools. The curriculum materials in these schools frequently came from one of two sources: Bob Jones University Press (associated with the scandal-ridden university) and A Beka Book, a publisher of Christian books (now called Abeka). Between them, with the public's money, these publishers have taught our youth some amazing things, as reported either by Deanna Pan (2012) or by Alice Greczyn (2020).

For example, I never learned from the textbooks in *my* public school that "The majority of slave holders treated their slaves well." Nor did I ever imagine that "To help them endure the difficulties of slavery, God gave Christian slaves the ability to combine the African heritage of song with the dignity of Christian praise. Through the Negro spiritual, the slaves developed the patience to wait on the Lord and discovered that the truest freedom is from the bondage of sin."

I also didn't know that "The Ku Klux Klan, in some areas of the country, tried to be a means of reform, fighting the decline in morality and using the symbol of the cross. Klan targets were bootleggers, wife-beaters, and immoral movies. In some communities it achieved a certain respectability as it worked with politicians." I guess my education in New York State was deficient, since I never knew these things!

I should also admit that I didn't get an A in my high school algebra course, but I never thought that abstract algebra was too complicated to learn. Perhaps I was wrong. Previous A Beka protional materials have stated that "unlike the 'modern math' theorists, who believe that mathematics is a creation of man and thus arbitrary and relative, *A Beka Book* teaches that the laws of mathematics are a creation of God and thus absolute . . . *A Beka Book* provides attractive, legible, and workable traditional mathematics texts *that are not burdened with modern theories such as set theory*" (emphasis added).

Another analyst of Christian school textbooks, Rachel Tabachnick (2017), alerted me to some additional textbook teachings that I never suspected. I simply never knew that "Global environmentalists have said and written enough to leave no doubt that their goal is to destroy the prosperous economies of the world's richest nations" (Kirk, 1999).

Through Tabachnick, I also learned that children receiving their education in some Christian schools, *supported with public money*, are informed that gay people "have no more claims to special rights than child molesters or rapists" (Matthews, 1998).

Writing in *Salon* magazine, Wilson (2012) documents other outrageous claims made in these curricula materials, some of which are purchased with public money for Christian schools in the United States, although these curriculum materials are in use throughout the world:

- Only 10% of Africans can read or write, because Christian mission schools have been shut down by communists.
- "God used the 'Trail of Tears' to bring many Indians to Christ."
- It "cannot be shown scientifically that man-made pollutants will one day drastically reduce the depth of the atmosphere's ozone layer."
- "God has provided certain 'checks and balances' in creation to prevent many of the global upsets that have been predicted by environmentalists."
- The Great Depression was exaggerated by propagandists, including John Steinbeck, to advance a socialist agenda.
- "Unions have always been plagued by socialists and anarchists who use laborers to destroy the free-enterprise system that hardworking Americans have created."

Religious schools should not be subject to much state oversight—I understand that. But many such schools claim to offer curriculum compatible with neighboring public schools, thus allowing their students to move to the public schools should they or their parents request that. For example, it is not uncommon for students in Christian schools to transfer at 6th or 9th grade to a traditional public junior or senior high. Or, with a high school degree after years of private Christian education, a student might seek admission to a public college. Since student transfers like these are common, shouldn't there be more inspection and approval of the curriculum and instruction in private Christian schools? Shouldn't Christian schools, or Jewish, Islamic, *or any other religious school receiving public money*, be inspected regularly by some agency of the government so that they can be certified *not* to be teaching antidemocratic, antiscientific, and anticommunitarian values? We have enough strife in this country without paying for schools whose values and curriculum are antithetical to our increasingly secular democracy.

Am I overreaching? Perhaps, ordinarily, private schools should not be subject to public scrutiny. But what if they accept public funds? What if they teach age-inappropriate or antidemocratic content to their students? Shouldn't the public know this? Shouldn't *all* public funds be subject to some kind of public audit?

For example, Rawls (2015) cites an adult whose memory of 6th-grade instruction in a Christian school was still quite vivid. The teacher "passed around shocking photographs of dismembered babies to teach about abortion." Sometimes Christian schools compare abortion to the Holocaust. Other times, elementary school students have been taken to local and state abortion protests, even to national events in Washington DC. Some schools regularly take their students to abortion clinics to protest. Are public expenditures for activities like these appropriate? Shouldn't tax-paying citizens know what is taught and learned in schools supported by public funds?

Naturally, as part of their anti-abortion campaign, many Christian schools worry a lot about sex. So they pass along unsubstantiated claims about condom failure and the horrible and lifelong consequences of sex outside of marriage. It is often our public money that supports curriculum and instruction of this type. Should that be the case? Should the state, often with comingled federal funds, support schools with anti-abortion programs when most state courts have ruled that abortion is legal? I have absolutely no issues with debate about the morality of abortion in upper grade levels, but should schools be providing anti-abortion education for our youth with public funds?

Pregnancy, as might be expected, is often greeted with expulsion for girls at Christian schools. I certainly don't know anyone who recommends teen parenthood, but if it occurs, shouldn't the mother be helped, not thrown out of school? Wouldn't that be the Christian thing to do?

To accommodate the fact of teen motherhood, a public high school I visited proudly showed me a classroom-cum-nursery that allowed teen mothers a safe place to leave their infants while attending classes to earn their high school diplomas. In fairness, one might ask if that is a proper role of a public school. I believe, as do many Americans, that preparation for successful adulthood is the mission of our public schools—even if it entails these kinds of accommodations to keep youth in school and help them to graduate.

Another curricular question is this: Is it appropriate for American education to promote lessening tensions between nations and religions?

I think so. But public funds support Christian schools that teach "[T]he darkness of Islamic religion keeps the people of Turkey from Jesus Christ as their savior." They teach that "[O]ver 500 people saw the resurrected Jesus Christ, [but] no one witnessed Mohammed's supposed encounters with the angels." And they teach that Islam is "fanatically anti-Christian" (Greczyn, 2020).

Finally, I want to point out the almost unanimous call to end corporal punishment of minors by the United Nations and by psychologists and other social scientists. Because of this, I ask, should public money be used to support schools that still engage in corporal punishment? Sadly, both Christian and public schools, particularly in the southern United States, approve of and still engage in spanking, or "paddling."

Although physical punishment of children has not disappeared in contemporary times, it appears to be more prevalent in Christian schools than in public schools because many of them operate on the principle of "spare the rod and spoil the child." Codes of conduct for many Christian schools say *it is their obligation* to use physical punishment, citing Proverbs 23:13–14, among other biblical sources. There they are told "do not withhold discipline from a child; if you strike him with a rod, he will not die. If you strike him with the rod, you will save his soul . . ."

Thus the "rod," switch, or paddle, along with other harsh punishments to ensure proper childrearing, is recommended in many of the advice books for Christian parents (Berliner, 1997). So it is not surprising that more physical abuse takes place in fundamentalist Christian schools than in public schools. For example, in 2007, a Chicago Christian school was sued for injury and surgical costs *after forcing a 14-year-old boy to kneel in place for 9 days*, causing a hip injury. In 2011, a Christian school teacher in Orlando was arrested on charges of beating a boy at her home with a rusted broom handle (Rawls, 2015). And in 2015, at the Christian-based Zarephath Academy in Jacksonville, Florida, a cell phone video shows male students holding down a female student while her teacher paddled her in front of the whole class (Amiker, 2015). The horrible offence the student committed? Running in the cafeteria!

Conclusion: There are certainly debates to have about the admissions and retention policies, qualifications of teachers, and especially the curricula used in *all* our schools—public, private, charter, religious, or secular. We, the American people, believe we can settle controversial debates about issues like these in public forums. We rely on an open press, and we settle these kinds of debates through citizen voting, and in our courts. Public oversight of public funds is part of the American tradition.

Frequently, oversight of public funding is carried out by inspectors general. In fact, the first inspector general of the United States was appointed, in part, because General Washington had an ill-trained army for the task he had ahead. So our very first inspector general was charged with identifying an educational problem, and asked to rapidly fix it!

Now, literally thousands of people work for various offices of federal, state, and (occasionally) municipal inspectors general. Each is typically responsible for identifying fraud, waste, abuse, and criminal activity involving public funds, programs, and operations. But outside of the federal government, few inspectors general are devoted to education, even though roughly 45% of all state budgets and 45% of all local budgets are used to support educational activities (Hussar et al., 2020). Thus, there is little oversight of how educational dollars are spent, and some of that spending has turned out to be scandalous (Berliner, 2022)! Just as bad, I think, is that there is even less concern about what is taught and what is learned in secular charter and private schools, or religious schools that receive public monies. This is not how it should be. I certainly would rest easier if there were inspectors spending a bit more time in the field overseeing what is taught and what is learned in our schools, in addition to their worries about how public money is spent. In particular, I think we need to examine religious institutions receiving public funds, so that the public has the information needed to maintain Jefferson's wall of separation as best we can.

In fact, if I made law, I would see to it that no private school—religious or not—ever received a dime of public money! Such schools can too easily sow seeds of separateness, privilege, and dissension, hindering the achievement of one of our nations most cherished goals: *e pluribus unum*, making "one" out of our many!

NOTES

1. It is worth noting here that public schools frequently do spend our public money counseling such students and their families, while private schools frequently do not. It is a simple fact that all sorts of "problem" students, the more costly ones, not just the sexually active or pregnant, are frequently expelled from charter and private schools of all kinds, and sent to genuine public schools. Moreover, most charter and voucher schools frequently find ways not to accept special education students either. Thus, the public schools incur educational expenses that most charter and voucher schools receiving public money do not. So public schools face budgeting challenges that private schools receiving public money do not. Thus, when one hears that charter or voucher schools are more cost-efficient than "wasteful government schools," these facts must be kept in mind.

2. So common has been physical punishment that the precise size and thickness of the paddle to be used has often been codified, e.g., specifying the type of wood, length of paddle, thickness of paddle, etc. Moreover, there is a likely reason that paddling is more common in Southern schools. Severe paddling was used to punish slaves so as to not leave any scars. A whip-scarred slave was of less value than an unscarred one, because the scars indicated an uncompliant slave and/or a runaway slave. Severely paddled slaves, it was believed, obeyed their masters better—as is desired of children by many adults.

The Place of "Soft Skills" in the Ultimate Success of Our Children

My mother passed away many years ago, so I can now make a public confession about a crime she committed year in and year out. When I was young, she prevented me from obtaining at least one full year of public schooling. Surely that must be a crime!

Let me explain. Every year my mother took me out of public school for three weeks, the weeks following the Memorial Day weekend. Thus, every school year, from kindergarten through 9th grade, I was absent from school for the last 3 weeks of the school year. This meant that over time, I lost about 30 weeks of school, or about one full school year.

How did a loss of a whole school year hurt me? Not at all!

First, I must explain to you why my mother would break the law. In large part, it was to get me out of New York City as the polio epidemic hit U.S. cities hardest from June through to the end of the summer months. For each of my summers as a youth, my family rented one small room for our whole family in a very small rooming house. The dozen or so renters all shared toilets, showers, stoves, and iceboxes. Of course, in that kind of environment, all the adults, and we children, learned patience and negotiation skills! We had no choice.

The rooming house was filled with working-class families at a beach called Rockaway. It was outside the urban area, but actually still within New York City limits. I spent my summers swimming every day, playing ball and pinochle with friends, and reading. And then I read some more. I am sure that for kids like me, leaving school enhanced my intellectual growth and helped form a healthier personality. I was loved, I had great adventures, I conversed with the many interesting adults in the rooming house, I saw many movies, I read classic comics and even some "real" literature. I read series after series written for young people: Don Sturdy, Tom Swift, and the Hardy Boys, as well as books by Robert Louis Stevenson and Alexander Dumas. Being out of school helped in my development of what I now know of as soft skills—sociability with vastly different people of vastly different ages. I developed ease of conversation, love of reading on my own, and participation in sports and card games with peers and non-peers alike,

85

and as I grew a bit older and became a "soda jerk," I learned to handle both customers and money. At my teenage job I also learned responsibility and tolerance, as well as how to make one of the greatest egg creams in all of New York City.

As I write this, with so many children out of school because of the COVID-19 pandemic, and based on all the time I supposedly lost, I am able to make a prediction: Every child who likes to read; every child with an interest in building computers or in building model bridges, planes, skyscrapers, autos, or anything else complex; every child who plays a lot of Fortnite, or Minecraft, or plays noncomputer but highly complex games such as Magic, Ticket to Ride, or Codenames; every child who does extra practicing of a musical instrument, or completes home improvement projects, or learns to garden and cook because they want to, will not lose anything measurable by having stayed home. If children are cared for emotionally, read stories that engage them, have interesting projects to do, and have good stuff to play with and adult models to converse with, I predict that *no deficiencies in school learning will be detectable a few months after students' return to regular schooling.* I didn't say they wouldn't score lower on standards-based achievement tests—but I doubt if any aspect of their life was negatively affected if they had the kinds of experiences I just mentioned.

It is the kids, rich or poor, *without* the magic ingredients of love and safety in their family, books to engage them, and interesting mind-engaging games to play, who may lose a few points on the tests we use to measure school learning. Just lying about, watching TV, eating inappropriate foods, and engaging in violent video games probably will not help school performance! Sadly, there are many children in our nation, of all social classes, who are raised this way. But what if, for many other youth who have not engaged in the "normal" school curriculum, they really do lose a few points on the achievement tests we currently use in each of our states? Would it really matter? Probably a lot less than you might think!

For example, all of the National Assessments of Educational Progress—the vaunted NAEP tests—were considerably lower 1 and 2 decades ago. But guess what? Those significantly lower-scoring students gave rise to the remarkably powerful economy we had just before the pandemic began. So it is quite likely that today's students, even if they do score a bit lower than before the pandemic, will not hurt our economy at all.

It is true, however, that school achievement tests have some predictive power. They do predict some of life's important outcomes, such as income and occupational status. In fact, school achievement tests do even a bit better than IQ tests in terms of the accuracy of their predictions! Because of these correltions with some important life outcomes, many parents worry when their children miss some of the curriculum tested on the standardized achievement tests given in almost all American public schools. Parents want to be sure that achievement test scores are as high as possible, potentially helping their children to be accepted to better colleges and setting the course for rosier outcomes during their chidrens' adult lives.

But high achievement test scores and their predictive powers are not merely a product of intelligence, or raw ability. Those scores are a product of a good mind . . . plus! The plus includes: studying for the tests, reading widely, having interesting conversations with parents and friends, reading newspapers, conversing with interesting adults, learning responsibility while on a part-time job, and so forth. Responsibility for studying is a soft skill. Responsible students expect to study, and may even like studying. They may like books and thus read on their own, a lot, even under their bedcovers with a flashlight, as I sometimes did. They may hang out at the school newspaper, where they pick up social skills as well as some skills related to writing and writing to meet a deadline. They may join student government organizations and learn how to talk with or petition adults—principals, counselors, school board members, and such. They may join athletic teams and learn the social skills needed to be successful in team sports, as well as learning the importance of practice, observing, critiquing, sharing credit for wins, and empathizing when losses occur.

The soft skills that schoolchildren possess—learned at home, at school, on the street, or in team sports—seem to be unusually good predictors of success in life, *over and above achievement test and IQ test scores*. That is because the grades that kids get in school, and their scores on tests of school achievement, and even their IQ test scores, are all influenced by the soft skills our children possess. These powerful soft skills develop in our children *during* their hiatus from school, *as well as* when they are in school. It is these skills that we measure quite unknowingly when we use GPA and achievement test scores to make predictions about a child's future. GPA and achievement test scores are simply saturated with the product of soft skills, and it is these skills that give GPA and achievement tests a great deal of their predictive ability.

Think of it this way: Success in attaining school grades, and attaining high scores on achievement tests, are each powerfully influenced by soft skills: Is the student personable? Do they share well with others? Does this child help other kids with their assignments and help the teacher with classroom chores? Does this child read for pleasure? Does this child skip some homework assignments, or do them carefully and turn them in on time? Does the child turn in written papers on time and give their papers at least one edit before submission, or is the first draft all that is submitted? There probably has never been a student grade given, or a school test score achieved, that reflects intelligence alone. Ability plus soft skills are what students present to their teachers. That's why grade point averages and school achievement tests predict success in life better than do IQ tests alone (Borghans et al., 2016).

Investigators working for Mathmatica, the highly respected social science research organization, studied the relationship between academic achievement and some soft skills on some of the important outcomes in life *after* high school (Deke & Haimson, 2006). They used high school math test scores as a proxy for academic competency, since math scores typically correlate well with most other academic indices. The soft skills they examined were a composite score from high school data that described each student's work habits, measurement of sports-related competence, a prosocial measure, a measure of leadership, and a measure of locus of control (taking personal responsibility for one's own actions).

The researchers' question (just like that of every teacher and every school counselor) was this: If I worked on improving just one of these academic skills, or just one of these soft skills, which would give that student the biggest bang for the buck as they move on with their lives?

Let me quote their results:

> Increasing math test scores had the largest effect on earnings for a plurality of the students, *but most students benefited more from improving one of the nonacademic competencies*. For example, with respect to earnings eight years after high school, increasing math test scores would have been most effective for just 33 percent of students, *but 67 percent would have benefited more from improving a nonacademic competency*. Many students would have secured the largest earnings benefit from improvements in locus of control (taking personal responsibility) (30 percent), and sports-related competencies (20 percent). Similarly, for most students, *improving one of the nonacademic competencies would have had a larger effect than better math scores on their chances of enrolling in and completing a postsecondary program.* (Deke & Haimson, 2006, p. 2, emphasis added)

This was not new. Almost 50 years ago, researchers on the political left pointed out that an individual's *non*cognitive behaviors were perhaps more important than their cognitive skills in determining the kinds of outcomes the middle and upper-middle classes expect from their children (Bowles & Gintis, 1976). Shortly after that, researchers closer to the political right found little evidence that cognitive skills, such as those taught in school, played a major role in occupational success (Jencks et al., 1979).

Employment usually depends on certificates or licenses—a high school degree, an associate's degree, a 4-year college degree, or perhaps an advanced degree. Social class certainly affects those achievements. But the latter group of researchers also found that industriousness, leadership, and good study habits in high school were positively associated with higher occupational attainment and earnings, *even after controlling for social class*. It's not all about grades, test scores, and social class background: *Soft skills matter a lot!*

Another researcher (Lleras, 2008), a decade after she had studied a group of 10th-grade students, found that students with better social skills and work habits who also participated in extracurricular activities in high school had higher educational attainment and earnings, even after controlling for cognitive skills! Student work habits and conscientiousness were positively related to educational attainment and this, in turn, results in higher earnings. It really is quite simple: Students who have better work habits have higher earnings in the labor market because they are able to complete more years of schooling, and their bosses in the real world are likely to value them because they get work done in a timely manner. In addition, the research in this area points to the importance of motivation in predicting earnings, even after taking education into account. As a whole, the studies in this area support the conclusion that the *non*cognitive behaviors of secondary students are as important as their cognitive skills in predicting later earnings.

Okay, so what shall we make of all this? I think poor and wealthy parents, educated and uneducated parents, immigrant or native-born parents, all have the skills to help their children succeed in life. They just need to worry less about their child's test scores and more about promoting reading and stimulating their children's minds through interesting games—something more than killing monsters and bad guys on a computer screen. Parents who promote hobbies and building projects are doing the right thing. So are parents who have their kids tell them what they learned from watching a PBS nature special, or from watching a video tour of a museum. Inquiry into what kids are doing by their parents and other respected adults is as powerful in shaping a child's interests, and at least as rewarding to those kids, as receiving something tangible as a reward for their behavior. Attention and positivity by teachers and other adults can shape the interest of a child—in what they write, what they read, how they play with others, how kind they are, how often they volunteer, how good they are at meeting deadlines, and so forth. Soft skills can be nurtured and developed.

Certainly, some of what we measure when we assess IQ is genetic. But skills like dependability, kindness, and sociability are probably much more influenced by environment, and it is these characteristics that influence a child's success later in life even more powerfully than do their scores on either an IQ or an achievement test.

So, repeat after me, all you test-concerned parents: *nonacademic skills are more powerful than academic skills in life outcomes.* This is not to gainsay for a minute the importance of, and the power gained from, instruction in literacy and numeracy at our schools, nor the need for achievement in history and science and many other courses. Intelligent citizenship and the world of work require mastery of a great deal of subject-matter knowledge. But I hasten to remind us all that success in many areas of life is not going to depend on a few points lost on state achievement tests that assess competency in any of these areas. In sum, if a child's stay at home during the recent pandemic, or their missing school for any other other reason, provides opportunities for the cultivation of soft skills, I have little concern about that child's, or our nation's, future.

A Plea for Multiculturalism in an Era of "Pop Culture"

Once upon a time, in an America before World War II, many teachers were woman of the upper middle class. It wasn't that their pay put them there; that was never the case! Rather, it was that they were the daughters and wives of accountants and pharmacists, of bankers and dentists, of engineers, professors, news reporters, and jurists. Those teachers were much less likely to be the wives and daughters of factory workers and farmers, or of clerks and tradesmen.

These teachers were generally the better-educated women in their towns and small cities, and they possessed that rarity in pre-World War II America, a college degree. They were generally from families with fiscal and intellectual resources because prior to World War II, it was primarily families of privilege who could afford to send their children, especially their female children, to college. Working-class children, in general, had neither the fiscal resources nor the inclination to go to college. While many of these more advantaged women didn't need to work, when they chose to do so, they often picked education.

These were frequently the kind of woman who took summer vacations in Europe before it became more affordable and thus more common to do so. In pre-TV America, these teacher-tourists brought back slides and photos of their trips, and in the classes they taught, they introduced students to the Louvre and the Eiffel Tower; they showed the changing of the guard at Buckingham Palace; and they intrigued their students with stories of the Tower of London. They also went to Washington, DC and New York City, frequently, for their husbands' meetings. And while in these cities they visited museums, attended plays and operas, and came back to their classes talking about those events and their adventures. In their own towns they were often active in book clubs, church affairs, PTAs, and women's clubs.

I am sure that my description is overstated. It is, however, an apt characterization of many of the elementary school teachers I had, many, many, years ago. The point I am trying to make is this: Public school teachers were once much more likely to be representatives of what passed for "high" culture in our society, and that is no longer as common. In 2022, neither teachers' pay, nor their status, allows most of America's teachers to partake of the "high" culture. Their class background mitigates against that, too. Teachers are no longer predominantly of the upper-middle-income classes, but much more likely to be from the lower-middle and working classes. In fact, even middle-class status no longer has the advantages of the lifestyle I described for the women who taught during the years when I was an elementary school student—a long time ago! Furthermore, instead of almost assuredly being the second income in a family, teachers now may be the sole breadwinner, and often with children to raise independently, as well. It seems to me that today's teachers, more frequently than in my youth, are representative of the common, mass, or popular culture, rather than what once passed for the "high" culture.

Before any of my friends and family jump all over me, let me say clearly that there is nothing wrong with that. In fact, if I were on a debate team, and my side had to defend the case for teachers being good representatives of the popular culture, I could probably do an excellent job. A powerful case can certainly be made for having teachers strongly attached to, or be representative of, the culture of the public school students whom they teach.

Teachers ought to be good representatives of the times in which they live, and they should frequently call their students' attention to prominent artifacts of the popular culture in which the teachers and their students are equally immersed. And if teachers were permitted and willing to examine the misogynistic or racial or political messages that are frequently found in pop culture, we should even be happier!

So I do believe that relationships with students are enhanced through the sharing of contemporary cultural artifacts. And that can only benefit the teacher-student relationships that are so necessary for good instruction to take place. And many of my generation may need to be reminded that today's representative of pop culture (for example, the free-form verses, jarringly nasal, and quite limited singing voice of a cultural hero of the 1960s) may well be tomorrow's Nobel Laureate in literature. This was, of course, what happened to Bob Dylan, who was so honored in 2016. And we all have seen how hip-hop morphed into rap, which is, of course, poetry, and which was soon woven into one of the most applauded and successful musicals ever to appear on Broadway: *Hamilton*. *Hamilton* is, in fact, a rap opera, little different in form from what is presented at the Metropolitan Opera House, a few blocks away.

But in addition to expecting teachers to help students navigate contemporary culture in all its wonders, I would also like to see teachers, and more broadly our schools, introduce our students to what is sometimes called "higher culture," though this is certainly not a good term, and one that I am unhappy to use. I want teachers obligated not only to teach readin', writin', and 'ritmetic, but also the world outside of a child's neighborhood, outside of their farm community, outside the bounderies of a child's familiarity. Kids should have some inkling of what else is out there besides what is in their local setting, or on TV, or coming through their earbuds and in their movie houses. There is a long cultural history of music, dance, theater, and art that should not be ignored because of the powerful pull of presentism.

Presentism is a problem. "Pop" culture is not the only culture that we have. In my view, if we are serious about *multi*culturism, we not only want to honor all races, religions, and languages, but we also want to honor *all* our cultural artifacts, many of which our students have neither access to nor appreciation of.

So how can our civic and education systems provide our youth with introductions to our "high" culture? How do we help today's teachers help our kids learn to dream about some alternative worlds to those in which they currently live?

First, we have to have educators recognize that *Star Wars* and *Julius Caesar* both have lessons to teach: Both are, in fact, morality plays and political tales, yet one is pop culture, and the other is high culture. In the hands of skilled teachers, both these productions teach the lessons many adults might want taught to our youth. But that requires skilled teachers, and neither teachers' status not their pay ensure that we will get great numbers of these kinds of bicultural teachers—the kinds of teachers I'd like to see more of.

Noble Lauriate and pop singer Bob Dylan, for example, says he was influenced as much by *The Iliad* and *The Odyssey* as he was by Lead Belly and Pete Seeger. That is exactly the kind of muliculturism for which I am advocating.

My personal multicultural outlook is evident in the fact that Lady Gaga is one of my personal favorites, and I have many of her CDs. But I also marvel at the magnificence of Dvořák's Symphony Number 9, *From the New World*, which not everyone knows has its roots in Black American and Native American themes. The grandeur of this symphony is, at its root, the celebration of our multicultural, multiracial nation. Lady Gaga can't top that, as wonderful as she is!

A symphonic poem originally titled *A Ballet for Martha* was written for a new ballet to be choreographed by the great revolutionary of classical dance, Martha Graham. It became a quintessential American ballet. Its score includes one of the most recognizable themes in our nation, because the melody came from a simple Quaker song called "Simple Gifts": Aaron Copeland's *Appalachian Spring*. Peter Gutmann (2005) notes that one of the great ironies in music is that Copeland—a reserved, openly gay, Jewish leftist with immigrant parents who was raised in Brooklyn—produced the sound many Americans instantly identify with the conservative values, vast landscapes, and the bold pioneer spirit of rugged American settlers.

Isn't there something inherently teachable in that? I think so, and so does Gutmann, who notes, "Every performance of *Appalachian Spring*—indeed, of any of Copland's populist works—proclaims loud and clear: 'This is America!'" So this composition, this composer, and this choreographer all should be subject matter for civics and social studies classes, as well as a feature of music and dance classes.

In our times, if our students are not exposed to these artifacts of what I am calling (for want of a better term) "the high culture" during their public school years, they may never encounter them. I think that would be sad.

But what might happen were our elementary and junior high students exposed to opera, ballet, and the symphony more frequently in our public schools? Will they be bored and doze off? Or will we be providing access to the wellsprings that a great artist of the future can dip into? And for those who worry about boredom, have you recently looked into an English class studying Chaucer or a civics class dealing with our Constitution? We support these curriculum units because we are certain that they are beneficial to our students—even as so many of our students yawn! *My argument about the arts is no different! Let 'em yawn! Like geometry, it could be good for them!*

Okay. I am reasonably certain that building a bit of curriculum around these ideas might trigger boredom among many students, and surely charges of irrelevancy are likely forthcoming from many students and their parents. Yet I believe that many other students might experience a magic moment in their lives. The ballerinas of the future need to see ballet, and in particular, those who are Black need to see Misty Copeland so they can see for themselves that after decades of prejudice against Black woman and men, someone who looks like them can rise to the very top of this art form. Black students need also to know the great artistry of Paul Robeson and Marian Anderson, who as part of the high culture were also part of the Civil Rights Movement that changed our country for the better.

Many students will need some coaching to learn how to listen to, and feel, the beauty of Marian Anderson's voice or a Mozart piece. I certainly did. But it shouldn't be difficult to get students to experience and understand the musical story told in *Pictures at an Exhibition*, or the triumph of Mother Russia over Napoleonic France in Tchaikovsky's *1812 Overture*. Just as Dr. Seuss and *Curious George* are read frequently to our kids before they strike out on their own to read *Charlotte's Web* or *Island of the Blue Dolphins*, certain symphonic pieces are good starters for appreciating the more ethereal beauty of Mozart or of the nonstoried form of symphony found in the romanticism of Beethoven. Surely, to build refined sensitivities to these overlooked cultural expressions that I am talking about, students will need some coaching to learn to listen to, and feel, the beauty of a Mozart piece, or to find the wonder and magnificence in the complexity of Bach, or understand the passion or comedy expressed in opera. But there are bridges: Romeo and Juliet's story is the same as that told in *West Side Story*. Hedda Gabler's life is a great reminder for today's young women that the independence they take for granted was missing in the lives of women just a few decades ago. What I am asking for is that school boards, administrators, and teachers find a bit of time to consider more than pop culture in what I know is now a very overcrowded curriculum.

Do we have the school time and the schoolteachers to do this kind of work? Not unless we choose to make these ideas a priority. And not unless we choose to have at least some alternatives to "presentism"—the underlying ethos that affects much of contemporary curriculum and contemporary life. We need to be assured that when state and local school boards debate educational priorities, someone from the fine arts community offers alternatives to the usual partcipants in curriculum discussions, often the leaders of our business community! They may not all be the citizens who should decide what is best to teach our youth!

Virtually all of us agree that learning what is useful in the world of work is a hugely important goal of schooling. Skills that lead to economic security, helping our students live productive and decent lives, has always been a rationale for the public funding of public schooling. There is nothing wrong with that. But let's face it: The pundits get the curriculum leading to preparation for work wrong, quite often. In reality, the skills needed for the world of work change much faster than a school's curriculum can ever keep up with. An example comes from my own life. To prepare me for the world of work that I soon would enter as a young adult, I studied woodworking, metalworking, linoleum printmaking, auto mechanics, and the fundamentals of electricity (by stringing a wire from a battery to a bulb over and over again, and for many weeks!). And I still don't know squat about electricity.

The skills I learned for employment in the manual trades—which working-class kids like me were supposed to engage in—are now seen as ridiculous. In fact, given my experiences, I have come to believe that the world of work can never be sensibly prepared for by our schools. In the real world, the future is a VUCA one: It is Volatile, Uncertain, Complex, and Ambiguous (Johansen, 2009). Educators do their best to prepare for that, but by ignoring a solid education in the arts—all the arts, contemporary and past, high and low, primitive and sophisticated—they are shortchanging our students of their uniquely human heritage. No other animal has music and art so intertwined with their behavior and their genetics. Why doesn't anyone on a school board notice that among the earliest dated findings of human life are artistic renditions? And has there ever been a tribe that has no music, be it drum, panpipe, penny whistle, or mbira? And what is a play but storytelling, also a part of human history, as far back as we can go.

So maybe, instead of focusing predominantly on preparation for employment in a VUCA world, we should welcome as a parallel activity preparation to live a life that recognizes the creative arts.

Both the new and our historic arts help students realize the beauty, provocations, and lessons that often reside therein. In fact, I believe that such a change is likely to increase the the quality of life of Amercian workers a lot more than do courses that prepare our youth for work. That is because work as we know it now is likely to change quite drastically in the near future, given the almost certain use of artificial intelligence to replace so many of America's laborers.

I wish that at state and local curriculum meetings someone would argue that you need the arts to round out and enrich the lives of all those students we prepare for gainful employment—and the quite real possibility for lives of little employment. Many of us have learned to get as much pleasure from watching a Raiders football team winning a game (may my wishes someday come true!) as we have had when Marin Alsop conducted the Baltimore Symphony Orchestra. Or we can get just as excited by our favorite TV show as we do when the New York City Ballet performs. *But first somone, in some educational setting, must teach America's youth how to appreciate symphonic works, classic jazz, ballet, fine and decorative arts, and the like.*

This is a difficult problem, even were educational leaders to agree with the general thesis of this essay. The popular culture and its representatives— our contemporary teachers—are constrained by their own socioeconomic backgrounds and by curriculum standards and tests that prepare our students for employability. No one seems to ask if we Americans might be better off if we prepared our students, as well, for a life engaged with the beauty and complexity of the arts.

Of course, not every classroom teacher can do what I argue here. And that is why we invented specialists: music teachers, art teachers, dance instructors, and particulalry school librarians. These all can be our designated brokers to what I am calling "high culture." But to ensure that our students are career- and college-ready, that they are capable of ever-higher test scores on standardized achievement tests, *we fired tens of thousands of these brokers of the fine and high arts, and this is really driving me mad!* The budgets for support of all these fired, laid off, or furloughed personnel are now used for testing, and technology to support testing, and I want to cry.

Impetus for writing this essay was when I learned that Los Angeles had recently cut its art teachers from 345 to 204, leaving an art specialist for 1 per 2,800 students! Los Angeles! A city where you might actually make a living in the arts!

Another article at about the same time informed me that Atlanta let go a batch of its music teachers. That Ithaca College discontinued its graduate Master of Music in Performance, Master of Music in Conducting, Master of Music in Composition, Master of Music in Suzuki Pedagogy and String Performance, and Master of Fine Arts in Image Text. Randolph Public School District, located in the Greater Boston, Massachusetts, region, cut their entire K–12 arts, music, and physical education (PE) programs and staff out of their 2020–2021 budget. Bah!

So I am convinced that we have defined multiculturalism much too narrowly. Its not just about acknowleging and celebrating Hispanics, African

Amercans, Amercian Indians, and many more Americans. Its not just about acknowledging and celelebrating Hanukkah and Christmas and Kwanzaa. It's also celebrating hip-hop, *Hamilton*, and opera; *West Side Story* and *Romeo and Juliet*; *Julius Ceasar* and *All the President's Men*.

Notice I am *not* defending the arts for their role in making students brighter, better test-takers, providing for employability, or even the likelihood of living a happier life. I am defending the arts, as Emerson wrote, because "Beauty is its own excuse for being." I am defending the arts because I believe in multiculturism. But multiculturalism has been defined much too narrowly for my taste! I want the pursuit of my kind of multiculturalism to help teachers and schools to remember that the cultural practices in every subgroup of society include fine art and ballet, opera and drama; symphonic concerts, jazz, folk music, ragtime, etc. The arts are manifestations of unique and historic human attributes that we possess. I want to educate this generation in the wide variety of these characteristics of our humaness, and without any concern for their economic impacts on our students and our nation. I'd like a few more voices to argue *Ars Gratia Artis*.

America Needs to Support Its Universities and Find Ways to Have Their Students on Campus*

In the United States over the last few years, enrollment in higher education has stalled or declined. Most recently, as I write this essay, some of that decline seems to be pandemic-related. But the drop in enrollment is also because the cost of colleges and universities has risen dramatically over the last few decades, while during that same time period the percentage of families able to afford higher education did not increase much, if at all.

The steep rise in tuition in recent years has a ready explanation: It is largely due to the disinvestment by states in their own universities and colleges. My state of Arizona is illustrative of many: From 2008, before the start of our last recession, to 2019, before the pandemic, Arizona cut its contributions to higher education 54.9% (Mitchell et al., 2019). When I first came to my wonderful university, I was impressed that tuition was relatively low, and it still is, relative to some other states, and also in comparison to many private universities. But it is also 92.4% higher than it was in 2008 (Mitchell et al, 2019), far outstripping inflation during that time period, which would have been about 21%. Like many other states, Arizona appears hell-bent on keeping its poorer citizens out of higher education!

There exists at least one other explanation for the enrollment decline, or plateau, as well. While higher education costs have risen, return on that investment for some college majors is quite limited. College majors such as early childhood, elementary, or special education, as well as the visual and performing arts, social work, theology and religious vocations, all pay poorly for many, many years after graduation.

The sacrifices that so many students and their families once made to obtain college degrees now appear to be less reasonable—as well as less possible. Students and their families rightly worry that the rewards of a

*A version of this essay appeared the June 25, 2020 blog post of Diane Ravitch, under the title of "The Value of a College Education in the Humanities": https://dianeravitch.net/2020/06/25/david-berliner-the-value-of-a-college-education-in-the-humanities/

university degree are less tangible, compared to what they were in previous generations. So incurring a large debt to attend college, particularly for those who may choose to be teachers, social workers, librarians, historians, or for those who major in literature, music, or art, seems simply not to be worth it. An uncomplicated cost-benefit analysis will easily support the idea that a university degree is not necessarily a wise investment.

The pandemic generated a shock to America's systems of higher education because many families, most institutions of higher education, and almost all of our American states are strapped for funds. The shortfalls in tax revenues throughout America's cities and states are likely to provide less revenue for the funding of our colleges and universities than usual. Under conditions such as these, enrollments in higher education are likely to continue to fall, and if that happens, universities will employ fewer faculty, provide students fewer majors and associated courses, and make universities seem, to some people, to be less valuable than they were before the pandemic. On this issue of revenue, and its side effects, Frank Bruni (2020), in the *New York Times,* noted, "our devastated economy leaves [university] missions and identities in limbo, all but guaranteeing that more students will approach higher education in a brutally practical fashion, as an on-ramp to employment and nothing more."

Would that matter much? If scenarios like these are likely, what would be lost? Really, what in the world does a university prepare one for? Isn't employability enough? That is the issue I address next.

*   *   *

When I was younger, working as the dean of the College of Education at Arizona State University, the university's administrative team was often forced to address these questions. We had to compare ourselves to, and try to determine our competitive advantage over, the still new but rapidly growing University of Phoenix, and its many imitators around the country. At ASU, we busied ourselves by greatly expanding our offerings and enrollments, hiring more and better faculty, and becoming one of the largest and best universities in the world, as recent ratings reveal (Shanghai Ranking, n.d.). We thought that our rise in international and national ratings would give us the competitive advantage over the private for-profit online diploma-granting institutions. None of those educational enterprises had the funds to support the bricks and mortar that make an authentic university campus, one that promotes campus life. But they too had a competitive advantage: cheaper and quicker degrees! So they continued to grow just as fast as we did.

In this time period, where there was enrollment growth at both traditional universities and at the online, private degree-granting institutions, Arizona's parents and legislators frequently asked us (1) what is it that we really did differently at our university; and (2) was what we did really worth both the taxpayers' money, and also the students' and their parents' money for tuition, and so much of the students' time? I tried to answer them with this: "At our university we make humanity—and you cannot put a price on that!" I then went on to explain what to many was my befuddling statement.

I pointed out that our public K–12 school system was, at least for the first part of the 20th century, designed for employability. But in the latter part of the 20th century, that system was transformed, and it began to emphasize preparation for college. Colleges and universities had then taken on the role of preparing their students for employability, albeit in better-paying and more prestigious fields such as medicine, law, business, engineering, and the like. University enrollments grew.

But the universities that welcomed the massive increases in enrollment from the end of World War II on had some centuries-old, fuddy-duddy traditions that were not an integral part of our K–12 systems, and were totally ignored in the private, for-profit, online institutions that began to challenge traditional colleges and universities. I use the term "fuddy-duddy traditions" deliberately. It's a term for a person or institution that is likely to be old-fashioned, traditionalist, perhaps conservative, sometimes almost to the point of eccentricity! In a way, as I'll explain, it is these fuddy-duddy traditions that give universities their *huge* advantage over a campus-in-the-ether—those quicker and cheaper, online degree-granting institutions.

Engineering, business, computer science, nursing, and almost anything else that was practical and being taught at modern universities became, over time, quite acceptable majors. That was not always true. Universities were once much more elite in terms of what they believed to be a "proper" major. But even as universities underwent changes wrought by modernity, they still wanted all of their graduates to have knowledge of the humanities—history, philosophy, literature, art, and music—and to learn, as well, something from the more contemporary relatives of the humanities, the social sciences . . . the *human* sciences! At ASU, we purposely chose not *merely* to teach nursing, business, engineering, computer science, and so on. Our fuddy-duddy academics aspired to do more than supply the economy with nurses and business majors, with engineers and computer wizards.

Quoting Berry (2009), I told interested community members and parents of those who might enter our university that "Underlying the idea of a university—the bringing together, the combining into one, of all the disciplines—is the idea that good work and good citizenship are the inevitable by-products of the making of a good—that is, a fully developed—human being."

Further, again citing Berry (2009), I told them that in particular, what residential colleges and universities are *"mandated* to make . . . are human beings in the fullest sense of those words—not just trained workers or knowledgeable citizens but responsible heirs and members of human culture. If the proper work of our public schools and universities is only to equip people to fulfill private ambitions, then how do we justify public support? If it is only to prepare citizens to fulfill public responsibilities, then how do we justify the teaching of arts or sciences? The common denominator has to be larger than either career preparation or preparation for citizenship. Underlying the idea of a university [is the idea of making] a good—that is, a fully developed—human being."

Some of our teacher education students, or their parents, wanted our college to be more like a trade school, emphasizing the teaching of this or that subject and how to do that "discipline" and write a good test. They all knew of schools that granted degrees in less than 4 years, where students studied only the minimum needed for employment as a teacher. But I always said to them that any other goal for a university than the full development of a human being, *especially for America's teachers*, was unworthy!

So I defend the humanities and social sciences for all students, asking that they learn more than just the skills needed to code, build bridges, or run an industry or a classroom. And I argue that the contemporary danger of too many fast-track teacher preparation programs is that the educators that they produce may not be the fully developed human beings to whom we might want to entrust our children. Here is one online ad for enrollment in a program to be a teacher:

> Meet——, someone who makes use of the partnership (with)
> _____University. Now, she's on track to earn her bachelor's degree in biology and her teaching license in under two years—all while saving tons of money, thanks to (our) low tuition (which is about half the cost of many other universities—or even less).
> College credit courses from an accredited university start at $49!

Here is what a three-credit course on ethics looks like in another online, degree-granting, and accredited institution. I imagine that if this course were taught correctly, it could prove indispensable for any business or education major. But is it taught in ways that might actually do that?

> The *Introduction to Ethics* course explores philosophical approaches to understanding morality and evaluating moral actions. In this course, you will learn about a variety of normative ethical theories, and apply these theories to real world ethical issues. With an understanding of the strengths and weaknesses of major approaches to ethics, you will build the critical thinking skills necessary to justify ethical positions. . . . No prerequisites. Self-paced. Students have 60 days to complete the course. (https://www.studocu.com/en-us/document/sofia -university-ca/ethics/sophia-learning-syllabus-for-ethics-course/20059225)

Do we really want an online *ethics* course to count toward a teaching degree? There is no discussion time allocated for this course. A student can whip through such a program in a few hours. And during that time, I am sure a student could learn the names of the great writers on ethics, and remember what they wrote, long enough to take and pass the exam in ethics. But can you really learn ethics without classroom discussions under a competent facilitator? Don't you need engagement with fellow human beings to learn what might be, and what might not be, ethical behavior? The course design also seems blind to the fact that there are many ethical dilemmas that have no genuinely right or wrong answers, which I should think makes web-based assessment quite difficult. I'll argue below that having real students on a real campus with instructors is not merely for the social experiences afforded (and the beer consumed), but for genuine intellectual transformation! That's exactly what the humanities and social sciences at the college level were designed to teach.

"So, what's a humanities?" Sam Smith (1979) asked decades ago. He answered his own question this way: "I can't really give you one answer. But I can give you several. It's asking *why* before we say yes. It's remembering something someone wrote two centuries ago when we can't remember what we wrote yesterday. It's mistakes we don't have to make because they've already been made and solutions we don't have to dream up because someone has already thought of them. It's how we got where we are and where we might go from here. It's things we can't measure, yet know have depth and breadth. It's parts of our culture we might lose like the Indian tribe writing its language down and putting it in a book. It's parts of our culture that we're often slow to recognize as such, like the legislature in Georgia finally making 'Georgia on My Mind' the state song and inviting Ray Charles to come down and sing it. It's the moral, philosophical, and historical issues hidden behind the political babble. It's rights and beliefs and their protection. It's preserving the past and the future and not just exploiting today. It's thinking as well as talking, questioning as well as answering. And it's placing human values and culture at the center of our world and making machines and technology and [some TV channels] serve us rather than the other way around."

The fuddy-duddy universities, in whose folds I have been wrapped for 50+ years, with their roots in the Middle Ages, now must address modernity, employability, fiscal exigencies, and the like. But as they do so, I hope that they continue to insist that the heart of a university—*whatever other activities in which they might engage*—are the humanities and the social sciences. It is from the university's offerings in these areas that we form fully developed human beings. And it is why we need students on campus, not taking their courses online, remotely and independently. It is highly desirable to have our youth enmeshed in a culture where the subject matters dealt with in humanities and social science courses are discussed in groups—whether in study groups, in dorms, or over beer at a pub. At least, for a few years, before our university students enter the world of work and full adulthood, they would be well served by living in an environment that values what is taught and discussed in the humanities and social sciences. That is why our colleges and universities need to stay open and find ways to keep students on campus. Offering hybrid systems online and in person allows students too much time away from campus, a place that has much more than classrooms, dorms, and food courts. And I will vociferously argue that programmed, online ethics courses are ludicrous! Such courses can only be dreamed up by a business major holding an administrative position in a profit-making institution of higher education that has its head in the clouds—if not up its behind! I cannot imagine any patron of the humanities who would design such a course!

As a contemporary example of the possible effects of the humanities and the social sciences on American society, I point to the protests that arose to demand societal change following the death of George Floyd in May 2020 (Harmon & Tavernice, 2020). A jury subsequently convicted a policeman of his murder, but before the trial there were protests across the United States and abroad. It was a worldwide, rare response to the white policing of Black citizens.

What caught my attention was that a close look at the protesters showed that they were not all Black, and sometimes not even majority Black. In our nation, protesters who were African American were joined by large numbers of white, college-educated citizens, in numbers that could not have been pre-dicted. The *New York Times* (Harmon & Tavernice, 2020) reported that in surveys of the protests in three cities, 82% of white protesters had a college degree! These are white citizens who are more likely to have been exposed to the humanities and social sciences than previous generations, and they learned in those courses what an imperfect nation we have, starting right from its hallowed beginnings and its fateful importation of America's first slaves, in 1619 (Hannah-Jones, 2019).

These better-educated, young, patriotic white citizens were compelled to stand with their Black sisters and brothers in working toward a more perfect nation. Their experiences in the humanities and social sciences may well be what leads college-educated students of all races to hold more liberal or progressive views, views that are more sympathetic to our nation's most recent outrages and the protests they inspire.

In fact, among people who identify as progressive, 67% thought that colleges and universities had a positive effect on our country. I think so too. But among those identifying with the more conservative side of our de-mocracy, those who lean Republican in their voting, 59% said that *college attendance was having a negative effect on America* (Fingerhut, 2017)! This is consistent with the views of one of America's great conservative heroes, Ronald Reagan. At a press conference in Sacramento on February 28, 1967, Reagan said that taxpayers should *not* be subsidizing "intellectual curiosity"! World-renowned universities such as the University of California, Berkeley and UCLA, he said, should shift their focus to teaching workforce entry skills! Perhaps Reagan forgot (as he was prone to do!) that there would have been no successful atomic bomb to end World War II, nor nuclear power plants for the production of electricity, without the UC Berkeley physics department of the early 1940s. And UCLA's nationally recognized hospital, which employs 30+ members of the National Academy of Medicine and over a dozen Nobel Laureates, along with its 30+ awards, suggests that UCLA, too, has something other to offer besides workplace entrance skills. It's what real universities do!

The effects of the liberal arts, the humanities, and the social sciences, accompanied by myriad discussions, disagreements, and heated arguments about the issues raised in university courses taken at a *genuine* university, really do change who we are and what we think about our democracy. That is why conservatives are quite right to be wary of our fuddy-duddy universities, teaching something above and beyond job preparation! Hundreds of America's old-fashioned institutions may actually have educated our youth in exactly the ways they intended!

But now, many of the institutions that actually did a pretty good job of educating America's young adults to be thoughtful citizens face a crisis. About the pandemic, Rosenberg (2020) argues that it is "uniquely and diabolically designed to undermine the foundations of traditional colleges and universities. [It does so because] we have pathologized closeness. Working side by side with a professor in a laboratory? Forbidden. Meeting with an adviser in an office to discuss one's academic future? Impossible. Living together, dining together, studying together, [arguing together]? Banned by medical advice and often by governmental edict." If students' personal interactions with others on a campus are overly restricted, the changes frequently brought about by the humanities and social sciences are much less likely to occur. To paraphrase Wittgenstein: A student who is not taking part in discussions is like a boxer who never goes into the ring.

It seems that the combination of taking courses in the humanities and social sciences, as well as living in a college community, produces graduates who are better-informed citizens: citizens who want to see our country move closer to its ideals; citizens who are more willing to protest injustice. And thus, our universities are graduating citizens more likely to bring about change. Are these improper aspirations for the college experience? And of all the college majors that exist, shouldn't America's teacher education programs be the most assiduous in wanting the humanities and social sciences to be a part of every teacher's university experience? Making humanity is what good universities do. It is a far more important goal for a university in a democracy than providing the specific coursework that develops our nation's computer programmers, business majors, architects, or teachers.

As Bruni (2020) noted before successful vaccines against the coronavirus were available, "A vaccine for the coronavirus won't inoculate anyone against the ideological arrogance, conspiracy theories and other internet-abetted passions and prejudices that drive Americans apart. But the perspective, discernment and skepticism that a liberal arts education can nurture just might."

We live in difficult times. But if we don't require a healthy dose of coursework in the humanities and social sciences, paired with a community of learners who discuss the issues raised in those courses, the times we live in will be even more difficult for us all. Universities need the money and the time with their students to "make humanity." If they do not get this, it could well mean reduced thoughtfulness and some shrinkage of caring in our society. It may mean fewer people to stand with those who protest injustice in hopes of making us a better nation. And that would simply be a shame!

Why We Need to End America's Apartheid-Lite Housing Systems Soon[*]

Parents often choose certain neighborhoods in which to live, hoping to enroll their children in schools that might provide their children with some educational advantages. As soon as I earned a decent salary, I, too, made sure my family had housing that gave us access to schools we thought might bestow advantages on our children.

It certainly wasn't hard to find data to support such common beliefs about neighborhoods and local school effects. But what I learned as a scholar is that school cohort effects—who you go to school with—are much larger than I ever imagined! School differences in student performance are real, and they are often attributable to differences in school funding, the quality of the school building, teacher and administrator quality and pay, or the differences in the quality of the curriculum. Those differences between schools are, to be sure, important. But it turns out that *who* you go to school may matter the most!

In most American school districts, particularly at the elementary school level, you generally attend school with those in your neighborhood. In the United States, in particular, neighborhoods are frequently segregated by social class, race, or national origin. This condition of contemporary life has taught us that public education in America works quite well when the population served by a school has the advantages associated with wealth and its correlate, a high level of parental education. Public education generally does not work as well when the population served has the disadvantages associated with poverty and its correlate, such as low levels of parental education, poor medical services, higher rates of minority status, and non-native-language-speaking parents.

What I have just stated about cohort effects is not a surprise to any thoughtful citizen, but what I share next are data on what happens to poor kids

*A version of this essay was published in the Horace Mann League Newsletter of September 26, 2023.

when they go to school with wealthy kids and what happens to wealthy kids when they go to school with poor kids. These data can directly answer the question: How large is the cohort effect that most people acknowledge as important?

As already noted, a belief in a neighborhood effect undergirds the desire of some parents to settle in certain towns or in some areas of a city and not others. Similarly, parents stuck in an economically poor neighborhood, or in a town that has fallen on hard times, are also right to believe that their children are not getting as good an education as the one provided by the schools that serve wealthier children. What appears to be less widely understood is that it is probably *not* the teachers, the administrators nor the paraprofessional staff or the counselors, and *not* the quality of the textbooks or facilities that give rise to this outcome—though without dispute, all of these are factors that commonly influence judgments of school quality. Instead, it may well be the nature of the cohort that distinguishes many high-performing schools from low-performing schools. The magnitude of the cohort effect is huge!

The evidence for my concern about the cohort effect comes from Australia (Perry & McConney, 2010). They have analyzed some of their achievement test data in ways that are different than we do in the United States. But there is no reason to think the Australian data would lead to any different conclusions were we able to do a similar analysis in the United States. To understand this large effect, however, requires that I create a small table. And if you are one of the millions of Americans who panic over numerical data and tables, relax; I think I can make it easy to follow.

One dimension of this table describes five categories of family income, the 1st through 5th quintiles of family income, roughly corresponding to "poor," "working class," "middle class," "upper middle class," and "wealthy." The average test scores of children in these five different groups will be presented.

For the other dimension of the table, imagine five kinds of schools. First, we identify schools that predominantly serve poor children. Next, we identify schools that predominantly serve students who are a little better off. Let's think of these schools as those that predominantly serve what we often call "the working poor." The next group identified are schools that predominantly serve students coming from the middle class. Next, we identify schools that predominantly serve the upper middle class. And finally, we identify schools that are attended, primarily, by children from wealthy families.

Of course, public schools almost always enroll students from homes that have quite different incomes. So there are usually a few children in schools that primarily serve poor children, who do, actually, come from wealthier families. Similarly, in schools that primarily serve the wealthy, we almost always find some children who come from poor households. That is what the authors of this study capitalize on to illustrate the power of cohorts.

Now, let's examine Table 16.1, The Effect of Student Social Class and the Predominant Social Class of the Students' Schoolmates on Achievement Test Scores. We have five kinds of students based on family income, and we also have five kinds of schools we identify by the amount of income earned by the preponderance of the families whose children attend those schools. I have constructed a 5×5 table, reflecting these five categories of student socioeconomic standing, and the five categories of schools based on the prevailing income level of families served by those schools.

This is the table we want to work with. In the middle cell I put the number 512. To interpret that score, look across the table and also look up: 512 is the average score on the PISA science test for a group of middle-income students attending schools that predominantly serve middle-income families.

PISA stands for the Programme for International Student Assessment. These are a set of tests assessing reading, mathematics, and science given every few years to dozens of nations, including both Australia and the United States. PISA tests are designed to yield test scores that average about 500 points. And sure enough, after these tests were scored, Australian middle-class kids who attend schools that predominantly serve middle-class kids obtained a score quite close to that which was intended to be earned by the average students of a nation. On the PISA science test, Aussie 15-year-olds received a score of 512. The data for PISA Reading and Mathematics tests show the same pattern that I share with you for the test of science achievement.

Now let me fill out the table with the PISA Test scores for all the other cells in Table 16.2, because they reveal something shocking, but not unexpected. They reveal what every parent already knows, namely, that cohort effects can be quite large.

Let's begin our analysis by looking down every column. We see that no matter what kind of families a school serves, the average scores of the students go up as the family wealth of the students in those kinds of schools goes up. Whether in schools that primarily serve the poorest students, or in the schools that primarily serve the wealthiest students, students from wealthier families outscore students from poorer families. This is well known. Social class, as determined by family income level, matters a lot.

Let's continue our analysis by looking across the first row. These are the scores of the very poorest students, those from families whose earnings place them in the bottom 20% of income. These are the students who usually do not perform well in the public schools of any nation. In that first cell, representing the scores of students who are poor, and who attend schools that primarily cater to the poor, the average PISA test score was 455. This is well below the average score of 512, which was obtained by middle-class kids in schools that primarily serve middle-class kids.

If we continue to look across this first row, we see that as the student body of a school changes, from one with predominantly poor families to

Table 16.1. The Effect of Student Social Class and the Predominent Social Class of the Students' Schoolmates on Achievement Test Scores

Individual Student's Socioeconomic Standing	The Socioeconomic Standing That Predominates at the School Site				
	1st Quintile/ Schools serve mostly lowest-income families	2nd Quintile/ Schools serve mostly low-income families	3rd Quintile/ Schools serve mostly middle-income families	4th Quintile/ Schools serve mostly upper-middle-class families	5th Quintile/ Schools serve mostly wealthy families
1st Quintile/Lowest SES students at that school site/ poorest students at the school					
2nd Quintile/Low-income students at that school site					
3rd Quintile/Middle-income students at that school site		512			
4th Quintile/Upper-middle-class students at that site					
5th Quintile/Wealthy students at that school site/The richest kids at that school site					

Table 16.2. The Effect of Student Social Class and The Predominent Social Class of The Students' Schoolmates on Achievement Test Scores

	The SES that predominates at the school				
Individual Student's SES	1st quintile, serving mostly low SES students	2nd quintile	3rd quintile	4th quintile	5th quintile, serving mostly wealthy students
1st quintile, Lowest SES	455	457	471	497	512
2nd quintile	483	493	501	528	540
3rd quintile	496	500	512	541	558
4th quintile	520	524	531	557	577
5th quintile, Highest SES	555	544	550	582	607

schools with students from wealthier families, *so do the average scores of the poorest students.* As noted, in schools that predominantly serve the poor, the poorest students' average score is 455, well below the average for the nation. But in schools that predominantly serve wealthy families, *this same population of poor students score an average of 512!* That is, when provided an education with a higher-achieving cohort, they achieve much more.

In fact, as a group, poor kids able to attend a school that primarily serves wealthy kids *achieve a score equivalent to the average for the entire nation.*

Poor kids who perform on tests at the average level of their nation is an outcome *never* found when we study schooling for poor children anywhere around the globe. Almost every nation wants its poorest students to do better in school. And here we see one way in which that might be accomplished: *Do not segregate a district's poor children by sending them to schools that primarily serve the poor.* Poor kids do better in schools that serve those from other social classes.

In fact, even without these data, this was exactly the conclusion of the U.S. Supreme Court, decades ago, when it found that separate schools for Black kids in America were not equal, and couldn't be made equal. Thus, they ordered desegregation of the public schools throughout the land. For the most part this did not result in more equitable schooling, as America's schools resegregated along neighborhood and township lines. But it helped some.

Let's go back to Table 16.2. In every row, as you go across this table, you see quite a large cohort effect. Whatever the income level of the students' families, if their children attend a school with a student body from higher social class families—a wealthier cohort—they do better on the PISA test. Even the highest-income families are affected, as seen in the last row. Students from high-income families who find themselves in schools that predominantly serve the poor score 555, an admirable score that is well above their nation's average. This demonstrates once again the power of social class in determining students' school success regardless of their cohort. But still, cohort matters! Look down that row to see how the cohort that a child goes to school with affects a student's scores! In schools that predominantly teach students from high income families, that is, in the schools that enroll higher social class students—those from the wealthiest families—the average score is 607. So, as a group, wealthy kids in schools that serve the poor do just fine, given the nation's average score. But those same kinds of kids knock your socks off if they go to school with other wealthy kids!

Looking at social class differences, from lowest to highest, in any of the five columns, we see about a 100-point difference in achievement scores between the students from low-income families and those from high-income families, regardless of the type of school they attend. The social class status of students is a powerful force affecting the outcomes of education, independent of the school. Research has consistently verified this common belief.

But now comes the reason for this essay: Let's look across each row at the scores obtained by students in different types of schools, from those that serve the poorest families to those that serve the wealthiest families. We are looking for a pattern. What we see is that students from any level of family income gain over 50 points on the test as they go from schools that serve the poorest students to schools that serve the wealthiest students. That's the cohort effect!

On this exam, the cohort effect is about 50 points. This suggests that if a child is in a school that serves the poorest students, and you can get that child to a school that serves the wealthiest students, that child is likely to score approximately 50 points higher on exams like the PISA. That's a lot. In a U.S. context, with so much dependent on test scores (access to honors classes, access to gifted-and-talented programs, access to college), it means that *if* we can get a child to a school that generally serves a higher social class than that of the child's own social class, we are quite likely to see that child achieve a higher test score. Thus, that child is likely to have a life that is richer in opportunities as well as in the attainment of wealth. The cohort you go to school with matters a lot!

How can educators ensure that we use the cohort effect to help more students demonstrate higher achievement in our schools? Obviously, bussing is one such way. We can bus students all around our cities and towns and improve the chances that the schools they attend will be more balanced by social class. That is, bussing can provide school cohorts that are not of one kind, either poor or wealthy. Bussing has been attempted in many cities, but too often the wealthier parents rebelled. They usually paid a lot of money for their homes, hoping to buy access to precisely the kinds of schools they wanted for their children. A monied middle and upper class typically want the advantages they can provide for their children to take precedent over the greater benefits that would accrue to the whole community by having schools less homogenous in social class.

The motives of these people may not be racist. They may, instead, be merely self-interested—wanting for their own kids something that isn't available to all kids—though the greater society suffers. But whatever their motive, it is quite clear that building school systems to reflect *their* priorities hurts our society.

Still another way to improve educational outcomes for lower-income youth is to build low- and middle-income housing in neighborhoods that now do not support such accommodations. That, too, is resisted by many parents. Sadly, America's housing system is, as Jonathan Kozol (2005) noted, an "apartheid-lite" system. It's not the apartheid system that characterized South Africa, in which classes and races were kept apart by law. But America has characteristics of that system, maintained by zoning laws, mortgage lenders, and those in real estate sales. We have developed an "apartheid-lite" system that keeps the poor and Black, Hispanic, and immigrant families from mingling with the wealthy in many of our towns and cities. But even more concerning to me is that it keeps their children from greater educational achievement.

A postscript: A related, and newer, study (Borman & Dowling, 2010) reanalyzed the famous report of the 1960s by James Coleman and his colleagues (1966). Coleman found quite small school cohort effects on student achievement, finding instead quite large family effects. The conclusion then was that family poverty (or wealth) mattered much more than did schools in determining the life chances of America's youth. Schools, it seemed, had little power to affect the destinies of children because family fiscal resources overwhelmingly determined a child's outcomes in life. If you look down each column of Table 16.2, you see what Coleman found: family income matters.

But this newer analysis of the Coleman Report refutes, quite vigorously, the conclusion that schools don't matter. Using newer statistical models unavailable to the earlier investigators, the more recent conclusion from Coleman's data set is that the effects of school were quite powerful, independent of the ordinarily powerful family effect.

Using different data sets, and different statistical models for analysis, the American data and the Australian data now reach similar conclusions. Family resources are very important, and everyone, everywhere, seems to understand that. But schools are very important, too, and it's not just the quality of the teachers or the administrators that makes for a highly successful school—though quality in these areas surely helps! Now we know that who is primarily served by the school matters a great deal, too. Thus, school catchment areas, school boundaries, and school admission policies all matter a lot!

To help our democracy thrive, our eyes ought to be focused on integrating schools by social class, and if we did that it would likely promote integration by race and ethnicity as well. American and Australian data suggest that the wealthier do not suffer any great loss of learning, or have less opportunity in life, when they attend school with poorer kids. But as Table 16.2 shows, while they may not score as high as they might have were they to go to schools with other wealthy children, they do score well above the average score of their nation, even when they are placed in schools that ordinarily do not score as high on these kinds of tests. Would wealthy parents allow for that? Probably not. And we know that forced bussing to mix social classes in schools has never been popular. This is one of contemporary America's problems.

It is not pleasant to contemplate, but when poor children go to public schools that primarily serve the poor, and wealthy children go to public schools that primarily serve the wealthy, then we approximate an apartheid public school system. It's certainly not the court-sanctioned racial apartheid of South Africa, but it approximates an apartheid system, *and we ought not to allow that to happen.* We need housing policies, in particular, that fight such a trend. Government can do that if we choose to allow our governments to spend some of our tax money for low-income and affordable housing in neighborhoods with more middle- and upper-income families. Segregation of the social classes—just like segregation of the races—simply will not yield a healthy democracy.

Premediation

A New Word for Educators and a New Technique for Helping Some Students Learn More Efficaciously

At an elementary school my wife and I were visiting, she expressed concern about the large number of students kept after school, apparently for "remediation." We asked more about this program and found it to be a program designed with the best of intents. Some K–3 students, mostly poor and frequently students of color, were having trouble keeping up with some of their classmates in math and/or reading. This is a common enough school problem when low-income students are in classes with students from higher social class backgrounds. The problem took on more urgency in this particular school because the teachers were extremely dedicated. They knew that if they did not help their students master the subjects taught in the early grades, the children might have a future of school failure ahead of them.

The teachers banded together and decided to help their students to do better by providing more instruction after school—on their own time and without extra remuneration! The commitment of these teachers to their students was impressive. We, of course, didn't think this was a bad idea, and thought, as well, that it was a noble gesture by the school's teachers. But as we observed the after-school classes, and thought more about it, we became a bit disturbed. Our concern was this: When a child must redo classroom work after school, it is likely that those singled out for such "remediation" learn to think of themselves as "slow" or "dumb." This cannot be good for the kids. Nor is it good for the parents of these students, who may then question their children's competence. So "after-school" detention of a child for academic reasons may have some unanticipated negative side effects.

Our reasoning was this: The good intentions of these hard-working and dedicated teachers may be undercut by eliciting negative feelings of worth among the students' and their families.No matter how we may choose to ignore it, or rename it, the root of the kinds of special attention we are talking about appears to be "remedial." And "remediation" is not a positive label for the description of the after-school academic work by these children.

Educators work hard to develop students' positive self-concept as learners. Remedial work, or whatever euphemism is used in place of that word, can be after school, or perhaps accomplished through special summer programs. But it is the "slower" kids who are involved, and they know it! Such a label shapes their self-concept as learners.

As we explored the topic of "remedial work" with colleagues, we learned that some folks thought that remedial classes might be the biggest roadblock to success for community college students (Watanabe, 2016). Under 20% of those college-age "remediated" students ever earn a skills certificate or 2-year degree within 6 years. Remediation, despite all the good intentions, apparently doesn't work as well as intended.

So with concerns about remediation, my wife, a former school principal, suggested adopting a policy of "premediation" instead. She thought that we should prepare the kids *before* instruction. In this way they may not be seen as the classroom "dummies," but might actually gain enough knowledge to have a leg up on the other students in the class! Teachers, instead of remediating the students because they didn't understand something, would prepare some of the lower-achieving students *in advance* of the lessons that the teachers were soon going to teach. Such an event seemed likely to help the students' self-concept as a school learner and was thought, as well, likely to improve their classroom learning.

I immediately thought about two lines of research in my field of educational psychology that supported my wife's intuition. First was the research on *prior knowledge* about a topic, when learning more about that topic or a related topic. Second, I thought about the studies of *time-on-task*.

Prior Knowledge: We know, quite conclusively, that those with the highest prior knowledge in an area learn the most from new instruction in that area. There is also considerable evidence that the more prior knowledge a student has, the quicker they can master new learning in that area (Tobias, 1994). So psychology provides a well-researched rationale for premediation. It turns out that when confronted by new material to be learned, "Those who begin by knowing less are less likely to be interested, less likely to generate their own learning experiences, less likely to sustain a sense that they have the ability to succeed, less likely to engage in knowledge-enhancing interactions with their peers, and more likely to come from a cultural background that is dysfunctional in the classroom."

So trying to teach the procedures and concepts that are required to be learned *before* the student gets them during regular classroom instruction is backed by sound research. A student's prior knowledge, the knowledge gained without any threat of grades and without the likelihood of looking foolish in the classroom, helps enormously when learning the same or similar material in regular classroom environments, at some later time. Even if imperfectly learned during premediation, during instruction in the regular classroom a student's chances of being thought to be smart by teachers and classmates are increased, and the student's chances of looking ignorant are decreased. So the subsequent increase in learning if students have some prior knowledge about the content that is required to be learned seems to recommend premediation over remediation.

Time-on-Task: The second thing we know is that the amount of time a student spends on learning particular tasks greatly improves a student's performance on those tasks. It is simple: The more time spent during learning, the greater the resulting learning. This statement holds, as well, whether a student is learning ballet, chess, or algebra! The more time you spend in learning that is motivated by wanting to do better in a subject area—whether ballet, chess, or algebra—the better you will do in assessments of that subject matter. I studied time-on-task for many years, and as common sense would predict, the more time spent succeeding on tasks that are similar to those that are assessed, the more learning appears to have taken place. No big surprise there, but we found that there wasn't always sufficient time provided for some students to master the concepts or procedures they needed to know.

Remediation certainly does work for some students, some of the time. And, as an instructional technique, premediation should work in the same way—after all, both require spending time learning the tasks or content that students are required to know. But learning because you are found inadequate in regular classroom instruction is fundamentally, and certainly emotionally, quite different than learning material you have already studied and know something about because you engaged in premediation activities, and are therefore familiar with the ideas being taught.

There is considerable research to support the idea of premediation. A well-regarded New Zealand scholar, Graham Nuthall, reported significant correlations between the number of test items a student knew before trying to learn some instructional material began, and the percentage of unknown items that the student could then answer correctly while learning related instructional material. In other words, the more a student knows about a subject matter before the start of an instructional unit, the more new learning students acquired when engaging with newer content in that subject matter area.

And my friend Sigmund Tobias did a series of studies that included a pretest in various subjects to be learned. He, too, demonstrated that new learning was significantly greater the more that students knew before they learned the new material. So two respected scholars both did a series of experiments and concluded that the more you already know in a subject matter area, the more new learning you will acquire in that subject-matter area after studying it further.

All this suggests that **premediation** rather than **remediation** has much to recommend it. Premediation, where you experience learning in advance of what might be in tomorrow's lessons, and importantly, in a setting where you are not embarrassed by mistakes, is quite different from making mistakes in a classroom that subsequently leads a teacher to recommend remediational activities, along with other students who all have experienced problems in leaning. Premediation versus remediation is the difference between possibly having a leg up during instruction versus having your legs pulled out from under you in front of the whole class!

In sum, if schools are going to keep certain schoolchildren after school to catch them up, perhaps they may want to change what they teach them in the after-school settings. Teach them what is coming, not what they missed. Help those particular kids feel smart, not dumb, in their regular classes. So, let's hear it for a new word: Premediation—the preparation of students in advance of regular classroom instruction, such that they have familiarity with, and prior knowledge about, the concepts and processes of a school subject they are subsequently required to learn.

*   *   *

After consulting the research literature on this topic, we found that Nuthall (1999a) reported a .38 correlation between the number of test items a student knew before the unit began and the percentage of unknown items that the student learned during the unit. In other words, the more material that a student knew at the start of the unit, the more a student learned during the unit. This reaserch provided some support for my wife's suggestion, based on her instincts, which were rooted in her experience as a teacher.

Nuthall noted as well that "children who perform best are those who go into the classroom with a larger store of background knowledge" (Tapu Misa, 2004). Nuthall wrote that the more students knew, the denser the network of associations, the more they could infer for themselves. "The more detailed the information and connections that are stored in a knowledge construct, the more available they are for use in later recall and problem-solving tasks" (Nuthall, 1999b, p. 337).

Nuthall (1999a) also wrote, "It is much more difficult for students from other cultural backgrounds to acquire expertise in the same learning activities because they lack the cultural understandings that allow them to understand implicit purposes and participate in a way the teacher intends. Consequently, they attempt to use knowledge acquisition processes that are ill suited to the classroom or they attempt to work with inadequate or fragmentary procedures" (p. 247).

Nuthall (1999a) also wrote that "Those who begin by knowing less are less likely to be interested, less likely to generate their own learning experiences, less likely to sustain a sense that they have the ability to succeed, less likely to engage in knowledge-enhancing interactions with their peers, and more likely to come from a cultural background that is dysfunctional in the classroom. As a consequence, they both learn less and acquire less effective means of learning."

We know that lower-scoring students enter many classrooms with less prior knowledge of the subject they are studying, and with lower past achievement in reading, mathematics, and other school subjects. These deficits are highly correlated with the amount of new material these students were able to learn in their classrooms. In sum, the research all suggests that if the time can be found for *pre*mediation, it might have advantages over *re*mediation.

The End of the Year and the End of My Patience

Some Thoughts on Charity and Citizenship

I write at the end of a bad year, one deeply affected by the COVID-19 pandemic, and our initial and feeble national response to it. Perhaps because of that, dozens of charities were writing to my wife and me, asking for end-of-year donations. In line with our income level, we support many of these charities, quite generously, I think. This is as it should be, given our economic advantage. But these communications began to get annoying, as requests for donations from the same sources come back to us again and again.

But I didn't recognize some of the charities that found us this year. The number of end-of-year appeals seemed overwhelming, a likely result of more sophisticated computer-aided marketing schemes. I had two responses to the many requests for help that we received this past year.

First, amidst the appeals for wounded soldiers, families of slain police officers and firefighters killed in action, and support for the housing, food, and medical needs of poor people, were some appeals that made me suspicious. I always check requests from organizations I don't know with Charity Navigator or similar publications. These publications provide trustworthy data for evaluating a large number of charities—both the better-known and those I had not heard of before. One of the new appeals we received was about supporting veterans, which we have often been happy to do. But this particular charity, for the year before last, reported annual contributions of almost $10 million and paid its director $680,000 a year, plus expenses.

I am well aware that top executives are worth a lot of money, but it seemed pretty clear to me that this charity is not one worthy of my admiration. Their appeal for our funds, and their description about how they would use them, was well written—tugging at all our heartstrings, as is common. I am sure that lots of folks, out of their sense of decency, will send them money. Their donations seem not to be large ones—most in the range of $10–50 each. They are very likely to reach $10 million in donations again this year, meaning that good people, trying to do good things, are providing a very nice lifestyle for the CEO.

So the first reason I am writing this essay is to provide a warning. Check a charity's expenses! It's all recorded in their federal filings, a public document required to be submitted annually to the federal government by all charities. Oversight of charities is necessary because each of them almost always claims tax-exempt status, and they pay no taxes on the incomes that they do receive. Donors to those charities are likely to take a tax deduction for their charitable gifts. And we need some reassurance that their reduced taxes are because they do, indeed, give their money to causes that increase the general welfare of our nation. We want to be sure a charity is not providing a tax exemption to its donors while, because of lax oversight, being badly run, overspending on office personnel, or in other ways not contributing to the public good.

Fiscal records for charities exist, and we should check them before giving them our support. Sadly, too many charities function like current President Trump's charities, which the New York State attorney general found were used primarily to illegally benefit his business and political interests. To no one's great surprise, when caught, Trump made 19 separate admissions of guilt, acknowledging his personal misuse of funds at the Donald J. Trump Foundation. Ultimately, he was forced to donate millions of his fraudulently obtained donations to "legitimate" charities—not the illegitimate ones he apparently created.

But besides alerting my readers to hucksters like Donald Trump, there is a second reason I am writing this essay. That reason emerged after my wife and I thought a little more deeply about who was making all those requests of us. Many were appeals for financial help to aid families of slain police officers and firefighters, wounded veterans, hungry American children, and those who needed special medical treatment. We were asked to help solve an almost innumerable set of problems associated with modern living *in the richest country the world has ever seen*. As we talked about this year's plethora of requests for donations, we realized something that we had not thought of before. We realized that some of these needy petitioners are people that *we*, meaning the American people *in our entirety*, really do owe. And we owe some of them big-time!

My wife and I realized that we, as individuals, should *not* be responsible for helping a slain police officer's family, nor the family of a firefighter who lost their life, nor any of the people in these professions who have employment-related disabilities. My family should *not* be responsible for helping a wounded vet, nor their family, through charitable donations. My family should *not* get requests to voluntarily help the nation's police and fire departments to purchase the equipment they need to keep them, and us, safe. We should *not* be personally responsible for feeding hungry children, or seeing that they and their families have a place to sleep and a physician to see.

Neither our military, our veterans, our police and firefighters, nor our nation's children should be objects of our charity. They are either our protectors or our future, so we—*collectively*—owe them. It is our duty to invest in them, not let them or their families fend for themselves and hope for charity if they die, are wounded, or subjected to unhealthy environments.

We should all be invested in aiding these people through official government-provided channels, not letting them become dependent simply on our nation's goodwill, and existing through the kindness of strangers. Our military, police, firefighters, and teachers are society's defenders. These are the people who provide America's children and families with the safety, security, and skills we need for growing the next generation of productive citizens. But we all know that hungry, ill, or ill-housed children cannot really make use of the advantages offered to us all by the military, police, and fire departments of our nation.

The care of veterans, police officers, firefighters, and all our nation's children should be *our collective responsibility*. The help they might need should never be subject to the vagaries of charity. This is especially true of those last-minute heartbreaking charitable appeals for donations—one more heartrending than the other—that arrive in the weeks around Christmas. It seems that the best advertising personnel and copyeditors raise the most money for the charities that employ them, while many equally deserving charities seem not to have the resources to compete for our attention and sympathy in the season of our giving. Should we really have a school lunch fund or a school clothing fund for poor kids? Should there be special appeals for medical funds for school bus drivers and school cafeteria workers who are not covered by school district contacts in the same ways as teachers and administrators? Or should we pay enough in taxes so none of these citizens of, and workers in, our communities ever has to be the object of charity?

As I thought more about my emerging opinion about this issue, I checked online and discovered that in many surveys, the United States didn't rank very high in its charitable contributions. We were beaten in our giving by some much less wealthy nations. In fact, Indonesia, Kenya, Nigeria, Myanmar, and Australia were actually the top five in one of these surveys. Americans are generous, but much less so than many nations that are much less wealthy.

But I soon realized that American benevolence, in terms of the time and money devoted to charitable work, frequently occurs because of deficiencies in our local, state, and federal governments. Government in the United States does *not* provide what is needed for those who work for us, or for our most needy. We seem especially uninterested in our children, who will eventually be asked to run our society, and perhaps even to protect us were war to come our way again. Certainly, many Americans deserve our help, and in addition, many deserve our thanks as well—such as the surviving spouses and children of those who lost their lives, or were injured while protecting the rest of us. I thought about our common fate, and of the common decency among my friends and neighbors. And I came to the realization that the needs of some of our fellow citizens ought to be our collective responsibility. Funds for such help should be paid for through our taxes—and certainly not through the funds collected by charities.

For the military, we need to allocate more money to the Department of Veterans Affairs or similar agencies. They can use those funds for hiring more field agents to be sure those who have been wounded can have decent lives. State and city social workers can serve in a similar role for those hurt while serving in our police and fire departments, as EMTs, as prison guards and trash collectors. None of our fellow citizens should lose a decent standard of living because they were hurt working for the common good!

We all know, of course, that money cannot replace lives, or heal the changes in lives that come with amputations, blindness, night terrors, serious burns, or the like. But money really does alleviate some of the problems associated with those conditions. And a more just monetary policy can convey our thanks for making the lives of ordinary Americans more secure. Among those who have served the public good are our park rangers, teachers, police and firefighters, EMTs, school nurses, and others who have served the public. These folks are usually modestly paid during their working years and may not have the resources for a middle-class lifestyle after retirement.

As an educator, it pains me to find 30-year veterans of our nation's schools now living in the most modest of circumstances—certainly not luxury—but with fewer resources than they deserve after serving our nation's youth for 30 years or more. And shouldn't we Americans, while we examine the way we allocate resources, ask if there is any reason why any child in the richest country in the world is hungry or without medical care? Shouldn't we ask why we find a parent administering lower dosages of prescription medicines than recommended because they cannot afford to give their children full dosages? Shouldn't we wonder why there are families living on the street? Are these people not all our brethren? Should they all depend on the kindness of strangers, or instead be helped by *all* the people who should be grateful to them?

Those of us advantaged enough, and who do care enough to support charities each year, can find myriad ways to help make the world a little better. And each of us understands that there is likely no end of need in this world. But that doesn't excuse us from acknowledging that addressing some of those needs are our collective responsibility. The particular needs of many of our citizens should not be supported primarily by any of our individual benevolence—support that is dependent on the kindness of strangers! The people in need whom I identified should be supported by all of us, by *we*, the people.

Obviously, for needs that are determined to be our collective responsibility, we need to spend more money. Although I am neither an accountant nor an economist, it seems to me that a small surcharge on the taxes paid by all corporations operating in this country would solve a lot of the problem. It also seems to me that the money is available, since a November 2023 search of some corporations reveals, for example, that the total compensation for James D. Farley Jr., president and chief executive officer at Ford Motor Company, for the year 2021, was $22,813,174. A similar search revealed that in 2022, Arvind Krishna of IBM made $16,580,075 in total compensation. And David Zaslav of Discovery had a 2021 salary of $246 million.

I'd certainly ask more, as well, of the approximately 100 companies in the Fortune 500 that paid 0% in taxes in each of our most recent years. Each needs to pay more to the commons for the wealth their workers produced with the help of the education that their workers received, and the protections their workers—and all of us—receive from our police and firefighters, our EMTs, and our veterans.

A scheme like this, or something like it, will only work if we simultaneously demand that our state and federal departments of revenue hire many more auditors with expertise in forensic accounting. In my mind, state and federal taxation departments should hire hundreds more accountants and auditors and pay them appropriate and decent government salaries and wages. I would even go so far as offering these tax auditors an incentive: tiny bonuses out of the recovered monies from improperly or untrustworthy tax filings—such as those of the notorious Trump family. Even a small bonus might attract some of the best publicly minded accountants. The employee incentive system for recovery of tax revenue that I describe is needed because hundreds of highly profitable American corporations, and tens of thousands of high-income earners, have paid little in taxes on their huge incomes.

I am sure that economists and budget analysts can improve on the plan I propose. But the increases in revenue collected by the U.S. Treasury seem quite likely to cover the costs for what is needed to for us to reconceptualize our obligations to others in our country. It would certainly make this the kind of society in which I would much rather live.

Furthermore, investment of the increased revenue in the ways proposed is likely to result in huge reductions in poverty, in hunger, in disease, and in crime. The result of those changes is also likely to be accompanied by noticeable increases in living conditions, in health, and in greater equity for minorities—with no noticeable effects on either corporations or on wealthy families. When those increased revenues are distributed in the ways I suggest, they will surely increase individual and national happiness, the pursuit of which is enshrined in our Declaration of Independence.

Come on, America—we can do better. And instead of all those heart-rending pleas for help that come to me at the end of each year, our postal service can deliver more Christmas, Chanukkah, Eid al-Fitr, and Kwanzaa greetings from more friends and family, each of whom, like my wife and me, might be more thankful that all Americans are living better lives.

References

Aiken, W. (1942). *The story of the eight-year study*. Harper.

American Civil Liberties Union of Arizona. (2017). Schools choosing students. How Arizona charter schools engage in illegal and exclusionary student enrollment practices and how it should be fixed. https://www.acluaz.org/sites/default/files/field_documents/schools_choosing_students_web_new_logo.pdf

Amiker, F. (2015, March 9). Video shows girl held down, paddled in school. News 4 Jacksonville. https://www.news4jax.com/news/2015/03/10/video-shows-girl-held-down-paddled-in-school/

Anderson, S., Leventhal, T., Newman, S., & Dupere, V. (2014). Residential mobility among children: A framework for child and family policy. *Cityscape: A Journal of Policy Development and Research, 16*(1). U.S. Department of Housing and Urban Development, Office of Policy Development and Research.

Annie E. Casey Foundation. (2024, July 8). Pandemic learning loss and COVID-19: Education impacts. https://www.aecf.org/blog/pandemic-learning-loss-impacting-young-peoples-futures

Anyon, J. (1997). *Ghetto schooling: A political economy of urban educational reform*. Teachers College Press.

Au, W., & Tempel, M. B. (Eds.). (2012). *Pencils down: Rethinking high stakes testing and accountability in public schools*. Rethinking Schools.

AZ School Report Cards. (2020). 2019–2020 school report card. Arizona Department of Education. https://azreportcards.azed.gov/schools/detail/80409

Ballotpedia. (2023). *Voter turnout in United States elections*. https://ballotpedia.org/Voter_turnout_in_United_States_elections.

Berliner, D. C. (1997). Educational psychology meets the Christian right: Differing views of children, schooling, teaching, and learning. *Teachers College Record, 98*, 381–416.

Berliner, D. C. (2022). The scandalous history of schools that receive public financing, but do not accept the public's right of oversight. In D. C. Berliner & C. Hermanns (Eds.), *Public education: Defending a cornerstone of American democracy* (pp. 268–286). Teachers College Press.

Berliner, D. C., & Biddle, B. J. (1995). *The manufactured crisis: Myths, fraud, and the attack on America's public schools*. Addison-Wesley.

Berliner, D. C., & Hermanns, C. (Eds.). (2021). *Public education: Defending a cornerstone of American democracy* (pp. 268–286). Teachers College Press.

Berry, W. (2009). *Home economics: Fourteen essays*. Counterpoint Press.

Björklund, A., Eriksson, T., Jäntti, M., & Osterbacha, E. (2002). Brother correlations in earnings in Denmark, Finland, Norway and Sweden compared to the

United States. *Journal of Population Economics, 15*(4), 757–772. doi: 10.1007/s001480100095

Borghans, L., Golsteyn, B. H. H., Heckman, J. J., & Humphries, J. E. (2016, November). What grades and achievement tests measure. *Proceedings of the National Academy of Sciences, 113*(47), 13354–13359. doi: 10.1073/pnas.1601135113

Borman, G. D., & Dowling, M. (2010). Schools and inequality: A multilevel analysis of Coleman's equality of educational opportunity data. *Teachers College Record, 112*(5), 1201–1246.

Bowles, S., & Gintis, H. (1976). *Schooling in capitalist America.* Basic Books.

Bridgeland, J. M., DiIulio, J. J. Jr., & Morison, K. B. (2006). *The silent epidemic: Perspectives of high school dropouts.* A report by Civic Enterprises/Peter D. Hart Research for the Bill & Melinda Gates Foundation.

Bruni, F. (2020, June 4). The end of college as we knew it? *New York Times.* https://www.nytimes.com/2020/06/04/opinion/sunday/coronavirus-college-humanities.html

Carrigan, R. (2025). Moving industry statistics. https://www.movebuddha.com/blog/moving-industry-statistics/

Casanova, U. (2012, April 13). The newest problem with graduation rates. In the Answer Sheet Blog, a column by Valerie Strauss in the *Washington Post.* https://www.washingtonpost.com/blogs/answer-sheet/post/the-newest-problem-with-graduation-rates/2012/04/12/gIQAwsH2DT_blog.html

Casey, M., & Rico, R. J. (2023, June 17). Eviction filings are 50% higher than they were pre-pandemic in some cities as rents rise. Associated Press. https://apnews.com/article/evictions-homelessness-affordable-housing-landlords-rental-assistance-dc4a03864011334538f82d2f404d2afb

Center on Education Policy. (2008, July–August). *Instructional time in elementary school subjects: A closer look at changes for specific subjects.* Arts Education Policy Review, *109*(6), pp. 23–27.

Chi, M. T. H., & Koeske, R. D. (1983). Network representation of a child's dinosaur knowledge. *Developmental Psychology, 19*(1), 29–39. https://doi.org/10.1037/0012-1649.19.1.29

Clotfelter, C. T., Ladd, H. F., & Vigdor, J. L. (2010). Teacher credentials and student achievement in high school: A cross-subject analysis with student fixed effects. *Journal of Human Resources, 45*(3), 655–681.

Coleman, J. S., Campbell, E. Q., Hobson, C. J., McPartland, J., Mood, A. M., Weinfield, F. D., & York, R. L. (1966). *Equality of educational opportunity.* U.S. Government Printing Office.

Corno, L. (1993). The best-laid plans: Modern conceptions of volition and educational research. *Educational Researcher, 22*(2), 14–22.

Crawford, J. (2006). A diminished vision of civil rights. Institute for Language and Education Policy. https://web.stanford.edu/~hakuta/Courses/Ed205X%20Website/Resources/Crawford%20Ed%20Week%20Commentary.pdf. A set of slides that illustrate Crawford's points is available at: https://www.powershow.com/view/293c9-YjY0Z/No_Child_Left_Behind_A_Diminished_Vision_of_Civil_Rights_powerpoint_ppt_presentation

Cremin, L. (1989). *Popular education and its discontents.* Harper & Row.

Daily Kos. (2022, December 23). The real reason for the attack on libraries. https://www.dailykos.com/stories/2022/12/23/2136462/-The-real-reason-for-the-attack-on-libraries

Davis, M. H. (2010). *Practicing democracy in the NCLB elementary classroom* [unpublished master's thesis, Dominican University].

Deke, J., & Haimson, J. (2006, September). Expanding beyond academics: Who benefits and how? Mathematica Policy Research. https://www.researchgate.net/publication/254430447_Expanding_Beyond_Academics_Who_Benefits_and_How_Princeton_NJ_Mathematica_Policy_Research

DeWit, D. J. (1998). Frequent childhood geographic relocation: Its impact on drug use initiation and the development of alcohol and other drug-related problems among adolescents and young adults. *Addictive Behaviors, 23*(5), 623–634. https://doi.org/10.1016/S0306-4603(98)00023-9

Educating for American Democracy Initiative. (2021). *Educating for American democracy: Excellence in history and civics for all learners.* Educating for American Democracy. https://www.educatingforamericandemocracy.org/wp-content/uploads/2021/02/Educating-for-American-Democracy-Report-Excellence-in-History-and-Civics-for-All-Learners.pdf

Egan, K. (2011). *Learning in depth. A simple innovation that can transform schooling.* University of Chicago Press.

Ericsson, K. A. (Ed.). (1996). *The road to excellence: The acquisition of expert performance in the arts and sciences, sports and games.* Erlbaum Associates.

Fingerhut, H. (2017, July 20). Republicans skeptical of colleges' impact on U.S., but most see benefits for workforce preparation. Pew Research Center. https://www.pewresearch.org/fact-tank/2017/07/20/republicans-skeptical-of-colleges-impact-on-u-s-but-most-see-benefits-for-workforce-preparation

Friedman, J., & Johnson, F. N. (2022, September 19). *Banned in the USA: The growing movement to censor books in schools.* PEN America. https://pen.org/report/banned-usa-growing-movement-to-censor-books-in-schools/

Garcy, A. M. (2011). High expense: Disability severity and charter school attendance in Arizona. *Education Policy Analysis Archives, 19*(6), 1–30.

Glaser, R. (1996). Changing the agency for learning: Acquiring expert performance. In K. A. Ericsson (Ed.), *The road to excellence: The acquisition of expert performance in the arts and sciences, sports, and games* (pp. 303–311). Erlbaum.

Goodman, K., Shannon, P., Goodman, Y., & Rapoport, R. (Eds.). (2004). *Saving our schools: The case for public education.* RDR Books.

Greczyn, A. (2020, June 7). Christianity's role in American racism: An uncomfortable look at the present and the past. Alice Greczyn. https://www.alicegreczyn.com/blog/christianitys-role-in-american-racism

Gutmann, P. (2005). Aaron Copeland: *Appalachian Spring.* http://www.classicalnotes.net/classics/appalachian.html

Hannah-Jones, N. (August 14, 2019). The 1619 project. *New York Times.* https://www.nytimes.com/interactive/2019/08/14/magazine/black-history-american-democracy.html

Harmon, A., & Tavernice, S. (2020, June 17). One big difference about George Floyd protests: Many white faces. *New York Times.* https://www.nytimes.com/2020/06/12/us/george-floyd-white-protesters.html?searchResultPosition=1

Harris, E. A. (2016, June 6). Where nearly half of pupils are homeless, school aims to be teacher, therapist, even Santa. *New York Times.* https://www.nytimes.com/2016/06/07/nyregion/public-school-188-in-manhattan-about-half-the-students-are-homeless.html

Henry, M., de Sousa, T., Roddey, C., Gayen, S., & Bednar, T. J. (2021). The 2024 annual homeless assessment report (AHAR) to Congress. U.S. Department of Housing and Urban Development, Office of Community Planning and Development. https://www.huduser.gov/portal/sites/default/files/pdf/2020-AHAR-Part-1.pdf

Herrnstein, R. J., & Murray, C. (1994). *The bell curve: Intelligence and class structure in American life*. The Free Press.

The High School Journal. (1942). *(7)25*, 305–309.

Hussar, B., Zhang, J., Hein, S., Wang, K., Roberts, A., Cui, J., Smith, M., Bullock Mann, F., Barmer, A., & Dilig, R. (2020, May). The condition of education. National Center for Educational Statistics. https://nces.ed.gov/use-work/resource-library/report/compendium/condition-education-2020

Jencks, C., Bartlett, S., Corcoran, M., Crouse, J., Eaglesfield, D., Jackson, G., McCelland, K., Mueser, P., Olneck, M., Schwartz, J., Ward, S., and Williams, J. (1979). *Who gets ahead?: The determinants of economic success in America*. Basic Books.

Jackson, P. W. (1990). *Life in classrooms*. Teachers College Press.

Johansen, B. (2009). *Leaders make the future*. Berrett-Koehler Publishers.

Jersey Jazzman Blog. (2017, July 20). When "miracle" charter schools shed students. https://jerseyjazzman.blogspot.com/2017/07/when-miracle-charter-schools-shed.html

Kini, T., & Podolsky, A. (2016, June). *Does teaching experience increase teacher effectiveness? A review of the research*. Learning Policy Institute. https://learningpolicyinstitute.org/sites/default/files/product-files/Teaching_Experience_Report_June_2016.pdf

Kirk, R. (1999). *Economics: Work and prosperity in Christian perspective* (2nd ed.). Abeka Books.

Kozol, J. (2005). *The shame of the nation*. Random House.

Kozol, J. (2013). *Fire in the ashes*. Crown.

Levine, D. I., & Mazumder, B. (2003). The growing importance of family and community: An analysis of changes in the sibling correlation in men's earnings. Working Paper 2003-24. https://www.chicagofed.org/publications/working-papers/2003/2003-24

Lipka, R. P., Lounsbury, J. H., Toepfer Jr, C. F., Vars, G. F., Alessi Jr, S. P., & Kridel, C. (1998). *The eight-year study revisited: Lessons from the past for the present*. National Middle School Association. https://eric.ed.gov/?id=ED454579

Litvinov, A. (2022, October 14). Out-of-pocket spending on school supplies adds to strain on educators. *NEA Today*. https://www.nea.org/advocating-for-change/new-from-nea/out-pocket-spending-school-supplies-adds-strain-educators

Lleras, C. (2008). Do skills and behaviors in high school matter? The contribution of noncognitive factors in explaining differences in educational attainment and earnings. *Social Science Research, 37*, 888–902.

Lubienski, C. A., & Lubienski, S. T. (2014). *The public school advantage: Why public schools outperform private schools*. University of Chicago Press. https://doi.org/10.7208/chicago/9780226089072.001.0001

Magic: The Gathering. (n.d.). Comprehensive rules as of August 7, 2020. https://media.wizards.com/2020/downloads/MagicCompRules%2020200807.pdf.

Martel, E. (2011). The Atlanta scandal: Teaching in "a culture of fear, intimidation and retaliation." *Nonpartisan Education Review/Essays, 7*(7): 1–7. http://www.nonpartisaneducation.org/Review/Essays/v7n7.pdf

Matthews, M. D. (1998). *Teacher's resource guide to current events for Christian schools, 1998–1999*. Bob Jones University Press.

McHenry, J. (1787). *Journal entry for September 18* [Archival material]. Manuscript Division of the Library of Congress.

Meier, D. (1995). *The power of their ideas: Lessons from a small school in Harlem*. Beacon Press.

Meier, D. (2021). If we believe that democracy is such a great idea, why don't schools practice it more? In D. C. Berliner & C. Hermanns (Eds.), *Public education: Defending a cornerstone of American democracy* (pp. 161–165). Teachers College Press.

Meier, D., & Knoester, M. (2017). *Beyond testing: Seven assessments of students and schools more effective than standardized tests*. Teachers College Press.

Milwaukee Journal Sentinel. (2018, October 5). Student turnover in Wisconsin schools. https://projects.jsonline.com/news/2018/10/5/student-turnover-in-wisconsin-schools.html

Mitchell, M., Leachman, M., & Saenz, M. (2019, October 24). State higher education funding cuts have pushed costs to students, worsened inequality. Center on Budget and Policy Priorities.

Nichols, S., & Berliner, D. C. (2007). *Collateral damage: How high-stakes testing corrupts America's schools*. Harvard Education Press.

Nuthall, G. (1999a). The way students learn: Acquiring knowledge from an integrated science and social studies unit, *Elementary School Journal, 99*(4), pp. 303–341.

Nuthall, G. (1999b). Learning how to learn: The evolution of students' minds through the social processes and culture of the classroom. *International Journal of Educational Research, 31*, 139–256.

Nuthall, G. (2007). *The hidden lives of learners*. Nzcer Press.

NYC Outward Bound Schools. (n.d.). Project-based learning. https://www.nycoutwardbound.org/select-strategies/project-based-learning/

OECD. (2021). Poverty rate (indicator). https://data.oecd.org/inequality/poverty-rate.htm See also doi:10.1787/0fe1315d-en

Open AI. (2022, November 30). Introducing ChatGPT. https://openai.com/blog/chatgpt

Pan, D. (2012, August 7). 14 wacky "facts" kids will learn in Louisiana's voucher schools. https:/www.motherjones.com/kevin-drum/2012/08/photos-evangelical-curricula-louisiana-tax-dollars

Perry, L. B., & McConney, A. (2010). Does the SES of the school matter? An examination of socioeconomic status and student achievement using PISA 2003. *Teachers College Record, 112*(4), 1137–1162.

Peshkin, A. (1986). *God's choice: The total world of a fundamentalist Christian school*. University of Chicago Press.

Ponzio, R., & Fisher, C. (Eds.) (1997). *The joy of sciencing: A hands-on approach to developing science literacy and teen leadership through cross-age teaching and community action*. Caddo Gap Press.

Potterton, A. (2013, November 1). A citizen's response to the president's charter school education proclamation: With a profile of two "highly performing" charter school organizations in Arizona. *Teachers College Record*. https://www.researchgate.net/publication/324569956_A_Citizen's_Response_to_the_President's_Charter_School_Education_Proclamation_With_a_Profile_of_Two_Highly_Performing_Charter_School_Organizations_in_Arizona

Qin, P., Mortenson, P. B., & Pederson, C. B. (2009). Frequent change of residence and risk of attempted and completed suicide among children and adolescents. *Archives of General Psychiatry, 66*(6), 628–632. doi:10.1001/archgenpsychiatry.2009.20

Ratcliffe, C. (2015, September). Child poverty and adult success. Urban Institute. https://www.urban.org/sites/default/files/publication/65766/2000369-Child -Poverty-and-Adult-Success.pdf

Ravitch, D. (2021, March 13). Success Academy charter chain ordered to pay $2.4 Million to SPED families. Diane Ravitch's Blog. https://dianeravitch.net/?s=Success+Ac ademy+charter+chain+ordered+to+Pay+%242.4+Million+to+SPED+Families

Rawls, K. (2015, January 12). 10 frightening things happening at conservative Christian schools that may be funded with your tax dollars. AlterNet. https:// www.alternet.org/2015/01/10-frightening-things-happening-conservative -christian-schools-may-be-funded-your-tax

Rosenberg, B. (2020, April 13). How should colleges prepare for a post-pandemic world? *The Chronicle of Higher Education.* https://www.chronicle.com/article /How-Should-Colleges-Prepare/248507

Rothstein, R. (2004). *Class and schools: Using social, economic, and educational reform to close the Black–white achievement gap.* Economic Policy Institute.

Sandoval, E. (2015, May 7). *Charter school closes doors without notice.* ClickOrlando.com. https://www.clickorlando.com/news/2015/05/07/charter-school-closes -doors-without-notice

Shanghai ranking. (n.d.). http://www.shanghairanking.com/rankings/arwu/2024

Shelly, B. (2017, February 20). Here's what it means when we talk about student churn in Kansas City. KCUR. https://www.kcur.org/education/2017-02-20 /heres-what-it-means-when-we-talk-about-student-churn-in-kansas-city

Simon, S. (2013, February 15). Special report: Class struggle—How charter schools get students they want. Reuters. https://www.reuters.com/article/us-usa-charters -admissions/special-report-class-struggle-how-charter-schools-get-students-they -want-idUSBRE91E0HF20130215

Singer, S. (2017, October 4). Top 10 reasons public schools are the BEST choice for children, parents, and communities. *Huffington Post.* https://www.huffpost .com/entry/top-10-reasons-public-schools-are-the-best-choice-for_b_59d541 cae4b0666ad0c3ca48

Smith, S. (1979, September 17). What's a humanities? Sam Smith's essays. https:// samsmitharchives.wordpress.com/1979/09/17/from-our-overstocked-archives -whats-a-humanities

Tabachnick, R. (2017, January17). Vouchers/tax credits funding creationism, revisionist history, hostility toward other religions. Talk to Action. http://www .talk2action.org/story/2011/5/25/84149/9275

Tapu Misa. (2004, May 5). Just because kids are taught doesn't mean they learn. *New Zealand Herald.* https://www.nzherald.co.nz/nz/itapu-misai-just-because -kids-are-taught-doesnt-mean-they-learn

Taylor, G., Shepard, L., Kinner, F., & Rosenthal, J. (2003). *A survey of teachers' perspectives on high-stakes testing in Colorado: What gets taught, what gets lost. CSE Technical Report 588.* University of California, National Center for Research on Evaluation, Standards, and Student Testing (CRESST).

Tobias, S. (1994). Interest, prior knowledge, and learning. *Review of Educational Research, 64*(1), 37–54. https://doi.org/10.3102/00346543064001037

Traub, J. (2000, January 16). What no school can do. *New York Times Magazine.* https://www.nytimes.com/2000/01/16/magazine/what-no-school-can-do.html

Trump, D. (2000). *The America we deserve.* Renaissance Books.

U.S. Census Bureau. (n.d.). U.S. movers and mover rates: 2018–2022. https://www.census.gov/content/dam/Census/library/stories/2023/09/why-people-move/figure-2-why-people-move.jpg

Veltri, B. (2010). *Learning on other people's kids.* Information Age Publishing.

Vogell, H. (2011, July 6). Investigation into APS cheating finds unethical behavior across every level. *The Atlanta Journal-Constitution.* http://people.uncw.edu/imperialm/uncw/PLS_505/Cheating_Atlanta-Teachers_7_5_11.pdf

Watanabe, T. (2016, November 14). Remedial classes might be the biggest roadblock to success for community college students. *Los Angeles Times.* https://www.latimes.com/local/lanow/la-me-ln-community-college-remedial-20161109-story.html

Westerlund, J. F., Upson, L. K., & Barufaldi, J. P. (2002). No time for Venus flytraps: Effects of end-of-course testing on biology curriculum in two states. *Electronic Journal of Science Education, 7*(2). https://ejrsme.icrsme.com/article/view/7702

Wilkerson, I. (2010). *The warmth of other suns.* Vintage Books/Random House.

Wilson, B. (2012, June 19). Shocking Christian school textbooks. https://www.salon.com/2012/06/19/shocking_christian_school_textbooks_salpart

Wizards of the Coast. (n.d.). You are a Planeswalker. Magic: The Gathering. https://magic.wizards.com/en/articles/archive/feature/you-are-planeswalker-2008-07-25.

Index

About the Author

David C. Berliner was born in the Bronx, New York City, and attended public schools from kindergarten through high school graduation. He moved west at age 21, graduating from UCLA with coursework in psychology, sociology, and anthropology. His master's degree in psychology was from California State University–Los Angeles. He earned his doctorate in educational psychology from Stanford University, where he studied with some of the leading educational researchers in America. Berliner contributed to the research literature on teaching and coauthored a bestselling textbook in educational psychology, among other titles. He was elected president of the Educational Psychology Division of the American Psychological Association and president of the American Educational Research Association. Most of his career was spent at Arizona State University where he and his wife, Ursula Casanova, had faculty appointments. His daughter, BethAnn, had a career in educational research and his son, Brett, is a history professor at Morgan State University. Attempting to improve education in our nation is the family business!